THE IMPORTANCE OF COMMON METRICS FOR ADVANCING SOCIAL SCIENCE THEORY AND RESEARCH

A Workshop Summary

Rose Maria Li, *Rapporteur*

Committee on Advancing Social Science Theory:
The Importance of Common Metrics

Committee on Social Science Evidence for Use

Division of Behavioral and Social Sciences and Education

NATIONAL RESEARCH COUNCIL
OF THE NATIONAL ACADEMIES

THE NATIONAL ACADEMIES PRESS
Washington, D.C.
www.nap.edu

THE NATIONAL ACADEMIES PRESS 500 Fifth Street, N.W. Washington, DC 20001

NOTICE: The project that is the subject of this report was approved by the Governing Board of the National Research Council, whose members are drawn from the councils of the National Academy of Sciences, the National Academy of Engineering, and the Institute of Medicine. The members of the committee responsible for the report were chosen for their special competences and with regard for appropriate balance.

This study was supported by contract number 2008-2146 between the National Academy of Sciences and the William and Flora Hewlett Foundation. Any opinions, findings, conclusions, or recommendations expressed in this publication are those of the author(s) and do not necessarily reflect the view of the organizations or agencies that provided support for this project.

International Standard Book Number-13: 978-0-309-16300-2
International Standard Book Number-10: 0-309-16300-5

Additional copies of this report are available from National Academies Press, 500 Fifth Street, N.W., Lockbox 285, Washington, D.C. 20055; (800) 624-6242 or (202) 334-3313 (in the Washington metropolitan area); Internet, http://www.nap.edu.

Printed in the United States of America

Suggested citation: National Research Council. (2011). *The Importance of Common Metrics for Advancing Social Science Theory and Research: A Workshop Summary.* Rose Maria Li, Rapporteur. Committee on Advancing Social Science Theory: The Importance of Common Metrics. Committee on Social Science Evidence for Use. Division of Behavioral and Social Sciences and Education. Washington, DC: The National Academies Press.

THE NATIONAL ACADEMIES
Advisers to the Nation on Science, Engineering, and Medicine

The **National Academy of Sciences** is a private, nonprofit, self-perpetuating society of distinguished scholars engaged in scientific and engineering research, dedicated to the furtherance of science and technology and to their use for the general welfare. Upon the authority of the charter granted to it by the Congress in 1863, the Academy has a mandate that requires it to advise the federal government on scientific and technical matters. Dr. Ralph J. Cicerone is president of the National Academy of Sciences.

The **National Academy of Engineering** was established in 1964, under the charter of the National Academy of Sciences, as a parallel organization of outstanding engineers. It is autonomous in its administration and in the selection of its members, sharing with the National Academy of Sciences the responsibility for advising the federal government. The National Academy of Engineering also sponsors engineering programs aimed at meeting national needs, encourages education and research, and recognizes the superior achievements of engineers. Dr. Charles M. Vest is president of the National Academy of Engineering.

The **Institute of Medicine** was established in 1970 by the National Academy of Sciences to secure the services of eminent members of appropriate professions in the examination of policy matters pertaining to the health of the public. The Institute acts under the responsibility given to the National Academy of Sciences by its congressional charter to be an adviser to the federal government and, upon its own initiative, to identify issues of medical care, research, and education. Dr. Harvey V. Fineberg is president of the Institute of Medicine.

The **National Research Council** was organized by the National Academy of Sciences in 1916 to associate the broad community of science and technology with the Academy's purposes of furthering knowledge and advising the federal government. Functioning in accordance with general policies determined by the Academy, the Council has become the principal operating agency of both the National Academy of Sciences and the National Academy of Engineering in providing services to the government, the public, and the scientific and engineering communities. The Council is administered jointly by both Academies and the Institute of Medicine. Dr. Ralph J. Cicerone and Dr. Charles M. Vest are chair and vice chair, respectively, of the National Research Council.

www.national-academies.org

Preface

In February 2010, the National Research Council (NRC) convened a workshop to investigate the feasibility of developing well-grounded common metrics to advance behavioral and social science research, both in terms of advancing the development of theory and increasing the utility of research for policy and practice. A planning committee was appointed by the NRC's Division of Behavioral and Social Sciences and Education (DBASSE) to organize the event, structure the sessions, select the participants, and ensure that the workshop would address the variety of research methods and data sets.

The workshop would not have been possible without the generous support and leadership provided by the William and Flora Hewlett Foundation. Marshall S. Smith, while at Hewlett, proposed the topic of common metrics as one in need of exploration. We are especially grateful to the planning committee members and other experts who responded to our request for background papers: Norman M. Bradburn, National Opinion Research Center and the University of Chicago; Nancy D. Cartwright, London School of Economics and University of California, San Diego; Dennis Fryback, University of Wisconsin, Madison; David B. Grusky, Stanford University; Robert M. Hauser, Division of Behavioral and Social Sciences and Education, National Research Council, Washington, DC, and Vilas Research Professor, Emeritus, University of Wisconsin, Madison; Rick Hoyle, Duke University; Robert T. Michael, University of Chicago; Geoff Mulgan, The Young Foundation; Robert A. Pollak, Washington University, St. Louis, Missouri; C. Matthew Snipp, Stanford University; John Robert Warren,

vii

University of Minnesota; and Robert J. Willis, University of Michigan. Their papers provided a substantive context for the discussions that took place at the workshop.

We also thank the many other people who participated as presenters, panelists, and discussants: Christine A. Bachrach, Duke University and University of Maryland; Kathleen A. Cagney, University of Chicago; Harris Cooper, Duke University; Sheila Jasanoff, Harvard University; Rebecca A. Maynard, University of Pennsylvania; Kenneth Prewitt, Columbia University; Barbara Schneider, Michigan State University; and Jack E. Triplett, Brookings Institution.

In the preparation of this workshop summary, we thank Rose Maria Li, who acted as rapporteur. In addition, Mary Lou Rife was helpful in the drafting of one of the chapters, and Christine McShane provided expert editing services for this report.

For a fuller list of sources on the topic than is included in this report, see the papers presented at the workshop: http://www7.nationalacademies.org/dbasse/Workshop_on_Common_Metrics_Agenda.html. For later versions of the papers, readers should contact the authors or look for a separate volume of the papers that is in preparation for submission to a university press.

This workshop summary has been reviewed in draft form by individuals chosen for their diverse perspectives and technical expertise, in accordance with procedures approved by the NRC's Report Review Committee. The purpose of this independent review is to provide candid and critical comments that will assist the institution in making its published report as sound as possible and to ensure that the report meets institutional standards for objectivity, evidence, and responsiveness to the charge. The review comments and draft manuscript remain confidential to protect the integrity of the process. We thank the following individuals for their review of this report: George W. Bohrnstedt, Research Division, American Institutes for Research; David S. Johnson, Social, Economic, and Housing Statistics Division, U.S. Census Bureau; and Howard J. Silver, Director's Office, Consortium of Social Science Associations.

Although the reviewers listed above provided many constructive comments and suggestions, they were not asked to endorse the content of the report, nor did they see the final draft of the report before its release. The review of this report was overseen by Cora B. Marrett, acting deputy director, National Science Foundation. Appointed by the NRC, she was responsible for making certain that an independent examination of this report was carried out in accordance with institutional procedures and that all review elements were carefully considered. Responsibility for the final content of this report rests entirely with the author and the institution.

We also gratefully acknowledge the contributions of Dorothy Majewski, administrative assistant; Mary Ann Kasper, senior program assistant; Kirsten Sampson Snyder, senior report review officer; Christine Maranto, Christine Mirzayan Science and Technology Policy Graduate Fellow; Catherine Freeman, who, as initial study director, helped in the development of the workshop; and Michael J. Feuer, former executive director of the NRC's DBASSE, for his leadership and support.

George W. Bohrnstedt, *Chair*
Miron L. Straf, *Study Director*
Committee on Advancing Social Science
Theory: The Importance of Common Metrics

Contents

1

Introduction

On February 25-26, 2010, a group of behavioral and social scientists met to explore the feasibility of developing well-grounded common metrics to advance behavioral and social science research. With support from the William and Flora Hewlett Foundation, the Committee on Advancing Social Science Theory: The Importance of Common Metrics planned and organized the event to gather information and examine the issues involved. The idea for the resulting workshop was suggested by Marshall S. Smith when he was at the Hewlett Foundation. He posed the thesis that one reason the social sciences have greater difficulty, relative to other sciences, in advancing theory is because they have less commonality among their metrics.

WORKSHOP GOALS AND ISSUES

The Workshop on Advancing Social Science Theory: The Importance of Common Metrics had three goals:

1. To examine the benefits and costs involved in moving from metric diversity to greater standardization, both in terms of advancing the development of theory and increasing the utility of research for policy and practice.
2. To consider whether a set of criteria can be developed for understanding when the measurement of a particular construct is ready to be standardized.
3. To explore how the research community can foster a move toward standardization when it appears warranted.

The planning committee considered a large range of issues in designing the workshop and selecting the presentations and participants. For example, it might seem as if the benefits of common metrics are obvious. Just as a common language facilitates learning and communication of knowledge for many purposes, so do common metrics facilitate cumulative and comparative research and its dissemination for policy, practice, and common understanding. However, the importance attached to common metrics varies tremendously across the behavioral and social sciences. In economics, there is a history of reliance on theory to define measures, although that is not always the case, and the development of standardized economic measures has accompanied the development of the idea of data in the public service. In the health field, a diverse set of morbidity-based indicators suggests that less arbitrary ways of summarization are needed, with the Patient-Reported Outcomes Measurement Information System offering a roadmap for the future. And in psychology, in the cases where psychological processes lack an overall theory, a reward structure has developed that tends to place a premium on inventing new measures for the same construct rather than encouraging the use of common metrics.

The benefits of standardized measures depend ultimately on their acceptance by the research and policy communities. Use drives measures in the first place and therefore whether they are standardized. Measurement must begin with the end in mind, and, if common metrics are the goal, then their purposes must be considered. That said, one size does not fit all. In this regard, it may be that a common metric per se, is not the ideal, but rather a few metrics widely used.

Another issue considered by the planning committee is that different metrics serve different purposes. When no measure is a candidate for widespread application, the use of multiple measures can help to triangulate a construct and to test the robustness of effects across different operational definitions. Thus, harmonization of measures might be possible when standardization is not. Scientists tend to favor harmonization because it reflects the competition of ideas, and persistent use is evidence of a measure's utility. Harmonization is seen as a form of standardization established *among* scientists, not imposed *on* them.

Although the original intent of the workshop was to focus on the importance of common metrics for advancing social science theory, in fact the discussion centered predominantly on how theory can inform measurement and on how common metrics can inform policy. Because common metrics require common concepts and construct validity, agreeing on an underlying theory is important. Sometimes theory is necessary but not sufficient for metric development in the social sciences. Often the lack of strong theories is reflected in the dearth of well-accepted common metrics. At other times, it is impossible to measure the variables demanded by the theory. A consistent theme at the workshop was the paramount need for theory as well as for a public policy purpose in motivating standardization of measurement for a particular construct.

Good theory and good measurement are often prerequisites for a standardized measure. Sometimes a measure is introduced and becomes popular and thus is accepted as the standard. Sometimes the need for or utility of a measure drives the momentum toward a standardized measure. Sometimes a concept is based on a theory that is widely accepted in the scientific community and that prescribes how the concept is to be measured. The ability to develop a standardized measure thus depends in part on the state of theory in different fields.

Although theory guides measurement for scientific purposes, political judgments often influence the development of standardized measures. The more consequential a measure is for policy, the more likely that politics will override science in establishing a standardized measure. And of course how a social concept, such as poverty or disability, is measured has serious policy implications. The standardization of measures is a social and political process involving negotiation. In some situations, what is measured may be less important than how it is perceived and classified. An example is the challenge of assessing change that involves not only aging but also the perception of the change with age. Skepticism often accompanies metrics that are generated from a process that is too obviously political. The integrity of statistical agencies is more easily maintained if the construction of measures is guided by accepted theories and is as resistant as possible to political and other pressures.

The social and political context of the academic community is another consideration. Even when there is benefit to standardization, the incentives to develop common metrics may be inadequate, especially in fields that tend to reward the development of novel methods, concepts, and constructs or new measures for the same construct.

Workshop participants had diverse ideas responding to the question of what the research community can do to foster common metrics when they are warranted. If the process of adopting an official standardized measure for policy purposes is transparent, that may create an opportunity for the scientific community to weigh in on its scientific suitability. Because common concepts and constructs are measured differently by different disciplines, it is important to learn how each one uses terms and interprets their connotations and denotations. Improvements in theory may come from greater interactions among the social sciences, as well as between these disciplines and others, with a movement toward greater interdisciplinary research. Agreeing on the type of data to collect could be another way of promoting common metrics. The use of common metrics also can be effectively encouraged by grant-making institutions as part of the peer review process and by journal editors.

Despite the interest in common metrics, some measures appear to defy standardization. As we have come to understand race in social and cultural terms, for example, the concept of race has become inherently difficult to measure, let alone in a standardized way. Measures may obscure important information in the underlying data or may fail to recognize the complexity of the dimension of interest. In such cases, data in their raw, disaggregated form are often more useful than when clothed in a composite measure or in meta-analysis. Both location and metric can affect comparisons; calibrating individual scales, such as with the use of anchoring vignettes, can help circumvent some of these problems rather than assuming a common scale.

Measures may also need to change over time, because concepts and what society considers important change. For example, the concept of poverty has changed over time, along with prices, products, and social norms—and a useful measure will reflect these changes. In health care, ignoring improvements in treatment would underestimate growth in medical output. And in recent years, there has been greater interest worldwide in measuring less tangible concepts, such as subjective well-being, satisfaction, and social connectedness, as well as a movement from single measures to indices and from activities to outputs and outcomes. And even if change is warranted, changing a well-established measure may be difficult, if not impossible.

Although the exploration of common metrics is to be encouraged, the meeting did sound a cautionary note on the prospects for useful and valid common metrics in the social sciences and the dangers of using imperfect or incomplete standardized measures to guide policy. Yet under certain situations, even an imperfect indicator can be good enough for promoting competent discussion about actions to take. However, concerns were expressed about the premature application of standards and the lack of appreciation for the role of successful science in generating standardization. Participants also noted that there is a risk that unnecessary standardization can mean that weaknesses get codified and reinforced over time and that distortions will occur from linking indicators too closely to policy decisions, particularly if indicators are meant to promote accountability. Common measures may also be lacking if there is no common understanding as to what the measures represent.

Although theory is useful in the development of metrics, some common metrics are not based on theory. An example is the unemployment rate, for which no economic theory appears to apply.

Finally, measurement breakthroughs can take a long time and require persistence, but the effort is well worth the investment. The development of standard metrics that are useful in theory and in practice is important and scientifically rewarding.

ABOUT THIS REPORT

This report is a summary of the 2 days of presentations and discussions that took place during the workshop. The workshop participants included the members of the committee that planned the workshop, along with invited speakers and a number of other participants. A complete list of participants is in Appendix A.

Report Limitations

It is important to be specific about the nature of this report, which documents the information presented in the workshop presentations and discussions. Its purpose is to lay out the key ideas that emerged from the workshop and should be viewed as an initial step in examining the research and applying it in specific policy circumstances. The report is confined to the material presented by the workshop speakers and participants.

A separate volume is planned of the papers presented at the workshop. Readers are directed to that compilation for a more nearly complete list of references than is included in this report. The papers in the form they were submitted for the workshop are available online at http://www7. nationalacademies.org/dbasse/Workshop_on_Common_Metrics_Agenda. html. Authors may have later versions.

Neither the workshop nor this summary is intended as a comprehensive review of what is known about the topic, although it is a general reflection of the field. The presentations and discussions were limited by the time available for the workshop. A more comprehensive review and synthesis of relevant research knowledge will have to await further development.

This report was prepared by a rapporteur and does not represent findings or recommendations that can be attributed to the planning committee. Also, the workshop was not designed to generate consensus conclusions or recommendations but focused instead on the identification of ideas, themes, and considerations that contribute to understanding the topic.

Structure and Organization

The organization of the report closely follows that of the 2-day workshop. Chapter 2 begins with an overview of measurement in the social sciences, followed by presentations on the challenges involved in developing common metrics and lessons from the economic sciences and the health sciences. These presentations provided a sampling of past experience with common measurements in both the policy domains and in terms of research on some of the core concepts in a diversity of social science fields.

Chapter 3 takes up the issues involved in indicators used for policy making and decision making, with examples drawn from the context of disability, high school completion and dropout rates, and race and ethnicity.

Chapter 4 focuses on social science constructs in the more basic social and psychological sciences. Social scientific examples of standardization range from qualitative classifications, like race/ethnicity and social class; to numerical scales describing psychological traits, social standing, or economic amounts; to normalized measures of the fit of statistical models and the effects of variables in such models. Three important aspects of standardization are identified: ontology, representation, and procedures. Examples are drawn from a number of constructs—including poverty, intergenerational mobility, and self-regulation—that highlight the obstacles to development of common metrics in the social sciences.

Chapter 5 summarizes the final discussion session of the 2-day event. The report includes two appendixes: Appendix A presents the workshop agenda and a list of participants, and Appendix B presents biographical sketches of the workshop speakers.

2

Measurement in the Social Sciences

In his overview, George Bohrnstedt (American Institutes for Research) provided a short history and review of measurement in the social sciences. He began by introducing measurement in the physical sciences and then discussed measurement approaches in the social sciences, touching in particular on seminal developments that have facilitated or impeded progress. He also introduced the topic of index construction, observing that indicators often turn out to be determinants of the construct rather than just reflecting it.

MEASUREMENT STANDARDIZATION IN THE PHYSICAL SCIENCES

Bohrnstedt made three observations about measurement standardization in the physical sciences:

1. Measures are social constructs, and the process of gaining standardization around measures is very much a social process involving social actors and negotiations, like any science or any political process.
2. Standardization is impelled along when there are strong commercial, political, or scientific forces at work.
3. Science has a strong, central role to play in the development of standards. An example of the adoption of standards as a social process can be seen in the way political and commercial interests worked against adoption in the United States of the metric system,

despite the involvement of scientists from many countries to lend scientific stature to the use of this measurement system.

Turning to physical measurements more generally, Bohrnstedt described them as characterized by standards that are based on strong theory and experimentation. In the physical sciences, theory is often viewed as a necessary precursor for measurement. With strong theory, measurements can often be used to confirm, reject, or refine hypotheses. In social science disciplines, the lack of strong theories is often reflected in the lack of well-accepted common metrics.

MEASUREMENT STANDARDIZATION IN THE SOCIAL SCIENCES

According to Bohrnstedt, there are some clear, tangible measures in the social sciences—such as birth, age, marital status, number of children—but the picture becomes murkier when one considers such concepts as attitudes, values, and beliefs at the individual or organizational level, or such concepts as school climate and organizational learning, or societal-level concepts, such as anomie and social disorganization. In the social sciences, it is often unclear whether the problem is the theory, the measures, or both. Bohrnstedt observed that researchers have not yet discovered how to define the kind of fundamental quantities in the social sciences that exist in the physical sciences. Social science concepts are large in number, fuzzy, and do not bear a simple relationship to one another, as is more frequently the case in the physical sciences. As a result, strong axiomatic theories against which to evaluate and inform measures are lacking. He cautioned, however, that it is not clear that social scientists would develop better measures if in fact strong theories existed.

Bohrnstedt traced the history of social science measurement, beginning with Pierre Guillaume Frédéric Le Play (1806-1882), who is credited with establishing what has become the modern-day social survey. He followed with mention of Guttman scales, popular in the 1950s and 1960s, which order both items and persons on a scale and are an important precursor to item response theory (IRT) scaling, developed in the early 1960s primarily to measure latent ability and achievement; application of psychophysical work on sensation and perception to attitude and value measurement using the method of paired comparisons; the scaling of attitude items, which led to development of the comparative law of judgment; the measurement of intelligence and the earliest factor analyses; the use of linear composites in the social sciences; and one-parameter Rasch models and subsequent two- and three-parameter models. There is increasing interest in IRT applications for the measurement of social and psychological latent concepts. One example is the measurement of health-related quality of life using the

Patient-Reported Outcomes Measurement Information System (PROMIS) at the National Institutes of Health (NIH).

Bohrnstedt ended with a set of ideas for constructing good measures in which the items reflect constructs:

- Define the concept as carefully as possible, specifying the domain of meaning.
- Use factor analysis to explore the dimensionality of the concept.
- After determining dimensionality, do a confirmatory factor analysis to verify.
- Estimate the internal consistency reliability of the measures constructed on the basis of the analysis.
- Fit the items for each dimension to a Rasch model.
- If the items will not fit a one-parameter or Rasch model, then fit them to a two-parameter model.
- Ensure that parameter estimates are invariant for various subpopulations.
- Develop new items to bolster sparse areas on the latent dimensions.

With respect to index construction, Bohrnstedt observed that in sociology, economics, and policy research, in some cases the assumption is that the indicators define the construct rather than the other way around. This is sometimes called a "formative" as opposed to a "reflective" model of index construction. Examples include an index of socioeconomic status, consisting of education, income, and occupation, and the consumer price index, which is based on a market basket of goods and services. The construct is in fact determined by or defined by the indicators that go into it. Typically, the indicators are simply unit-weighted, but in some cases they are weighted on the basis of theory, differential utilities, or other preferences (e.g., relative importance based on a community survey). One can estimate the weights of the indicators if there are multiple indicators and multiple causes (the MIMIC model).

COMPARABLE METRICS: SOME EXAMPLES

Robert Hauser (Division of Behavioral and Social Sciences and Education, National Research Council, Washington, DC, and Vilas Research Professor, Emeritus, University of Wisconsin, Madison) reflected on the tradeoff inherent in standardization. In the social, behavioral, and economic sciences, standardization of measures can help the accumulation of evidence because it permits valid comparisons across time, place, or units of observations (e.g., persons, families, settings, localities, organizations). Standardization also can create common understandings, when measurement intersects with policy. At the same time, however, standardization can entail the loss of information, and too much standardization may make extensive evidence uninformative and misleading. A delicate balance must be negotiated, he said, between standardization of measurement and validity of social scientific constructs. This can be complicated, because measurement can overlap with representation (who or what is being measured), analysis (how data will be described and used), theory, and policy.

Hauser then illustrated his point with a number of public metrics, in declining order of success, based on his judgment of the validity and usage of the measures:

- The *unemployment rate* is a social scientific invention based on a detailed behavioral report of job searching during a reference week by members of the labor force. It is defective in the sense that the officially unemployed do not include "discouraged workers," persons who have given up on their search for employment, or the underemployed. This defect is exacerbated when unemployment is high, as the measure underestimates the extent of economic distress.

- The *official poverty line* is a more recent scientific invention frequently used in policy applications despite major weaknesses that greatly limited its validity and usefulness from the outset. It is an absolute standard in real dollars, updated only to reflect changes in the consumer price index. Because of this and the fact that living standards and the share of food in family budgets have changed, the standard has become increasingly obsolete. In Hauser's estimation, the official poverty line has been overused in thousands of research papers and books, and perceptions about poverty and the poor would differ if a standard measure of greater validity were widely accepted.

- *Academic achievement levels* offer a more recent example of a nominally social scientific, standardized measure that has become visible and influential in public discourse and policy. Although drawn on questionable and subjective methods, academic achievement levels have nevertheless become ubiquitous in reports on diverse subjects at state and national levels. Public and political demands for understandable metrics of academic accountability have trumped their negative evaluations, he said. In this case, Hauser pointed out, the creation of a supposedly scientific set of standards led to their reification in law, to the creation of competing standards, and to comparisons of populations in differing but nominally identical metrics.

MEASUREMENT IN THE SOCIAL SCIENCES

- The 1992 National Adult Literacy Study reported five *levels of literacy,* based on four cutoff points set at equal intervals, without specific descriptors, that presumably indicate discrete breaks in competence. From this score distribution, it is not possible to determine the number of people who are considered illiterate in the United States. The National Center for Education Statistics, when it was about to undertake the successor National Assessment of Adult Literacy (NAAL) in 2003, asked the National Research Council (NRC) to recommend standards for adult literacy that could be used in the NAAL and applied retroactively to the National Adult Literacy Study in order to compare literacy levels across the decade among all adults and specific population groups. The NRC report *Measuring Literacy: Performance Levels for Adults* (National Research Council, 2005) developed five categories with explicit descriptions corresponding roughly to readiness for successive levels of formal education. The NRC report concludes from experimental work that the whole enterprise of line drawing is on very shaky ground.

- The *Voluntary National Tests* were a 1997 proposal of the Clinton administration for tests of reading at grade 4 and mathematics at grade 8 that became a dramatic and failed effort to create a common metric for the assessment of academic achievement and changes in it. The proposal was to give the same assessment to all students nationwide, and individual reports would be shared with students, parents, teachers, and school administrators. Advocates believed that this diagnostic information would increase motivation to improve academic achievement. Hauser said that the project ultimately died due to strong opposition from Republicans who believed it would destroy the traditional prerogatives of local school systems and from minority groups afraid it would stigmatize them. He mentioned two proposals by Congress for NRC studies to address measurement issues in ways that would permit this project to go forward without giving everyone the same test. The first one, to equate the scales of existing tests, was considered not feasible. The second proposal, to insert modest numbers of existing items from national assessments into existing tests on state assessments, also was rejected because of substantial differences in context or administration between the state and national testing programs. Hauser was struck by the fact that Congress directly addressed technical issues of comparability in measurement, at least attempting to establish national comparability in the measurement of individual academic performance in its proposals to the NRC.

Accumulating Evidence, Comparing Effects

According to Hauser, social scientific examples of standardization range from qualitative classifications, like race/ethnicity and social class; to numerical scales describing psychological traits, social standing, or economic amounts; to normalized measures of the fit of statistical models and the effects of variables in such models. He discussed social class, occupational prestige, and occupational socioeconomic status as examples involving the normalization of metrics.

Social class is a core concept of sociology. It is ubiquitous, yet there is endless disagreement about how to measure it. In recent sociological research, there have been three main contenders on how to measure social class: a neo-Marxist classification developed by Erik Wright (1993),[1] a neo-Weberian classification developed by Robert Erikson and John Goldthorpe (1992),[2] and variants of the Edwards scale, a socioeconomic classification of occupations by the U.S. Census Bureau that was developed in the 1930s. The Edwards scale captures a central hierarchical dimension of the occupational structure, but major classification changes in the Census Bureau's occupational system and the federal system more generally have made it difficult to maintain in any comparable form.[3] This system has a stronger empirical than theoretical grounding. The Wright and Erikson-Goldthorpe class schemes have a strong basis in sociological theory, but each also has notable empirical weaknesses.

All three classification schemes exemplify the strengths and weaknesses of common metrics. On the positive side, the schemes have been used extensively in cumulative and comparative research, as well as for social reporting. However, each of the three schemes competes with the other two, thus reducing the set of comparable studies and observations.

In seeing how well the three schemes compare, Miech and Hauser (2001) looked at health outcomes in relation to all three of these measures

---

[1]Wright's class scheme uses broad occupation categories plus distinctions of ownership, size of establishment, and supervisory and management responsibility. It has chiefly been used by Wright and his international collaborators and is a competitor to the Erickson-Goldthorpe scheme.

[2]The Erikson and Goldthorpe scheme uses many of the same ingredients but somewhat differently. It was developed for an international comparative study of social mobility, is relatively easy to construct, and is used much more than Wright's scheme, especially in international work. The problem is that it suppresses the main socioeconomic dimension that comes out so clearly in the Edwards scale.

[3]The Census Bureau follows the Standard Occupation Classification system, which is developed by an interagency group and agreed on by the Office of Management and Budget. This is an example of a standardized metric that changes over time to meet users' needs and the changing work environment. It is not the result of the federal system making changes, but a reflection of the changing economic environment.

in the Wisconsin Longitudinal Study. They found that if used in occupational classification to explain health differentials, the Edwards scale was really the best choice, yet a simple classification of educational attainment actually dominated any of the occupational components.

Hauser closed this discussion by raising the broader problem with the use of any of the standard measures of "social class": the belief that these, or closely related measures of social standing, taken alone, fully represent the social and economic standing of a person, household, or family. In his view, this simplistic view fails to recognize the complexity of contemporary systems of social stratification, in which inequalities are created and maintained in a substantially but by no means highly correlated mix of psychological, educational, occupational, and economic dimensions. He stated that this, more than the details of class measurement, is the greatest disadvantage of standardization in the measurement of social class.

Occupational prestige, based on lay or expert reports of the "general social standing" of occupations, was found in the mid-1950s to correlate highly across national populations, later across time, and between blacks and whites. Research by Donald Treiman (1976) produced the Standard International Occupational Prestige Scale. Hauser surmised that this scale did not take hold in part because sociologists around the world were more interested in the peculiarities of social mobility in their own nations and less concerned about comparability, as well as the fact that empirical research showed that prestige was not the main dimension of occupational persistence.

Studies of occupational prestige in the United States beginning as early as 1947 covered only modest numbers of occupational titles. In the absence of a complete set of prestige scores, Duncan created a proxy measure, the Socioeconomic Index for All Occupations (SEI),[4] which has been widely used in U.S. studies of occupational mobility, including intergenerational mobility. Hauser emphasized that the SEI represents occupational standing alone, not individual or family socioeconomic status. This measure and its competitors (e.g., the Hollingshead Index of Social Position, the Nam-Powers Index) all have limitations.[5] For example, all of these indexes are based on male workers alone, so they are not valid in today's market, in

---

[4]This was done by regressing a prestige measure for 45 occupational titles in the 1947 North-Hatt Study on age-standardized educational attainment and income of occupations held by men in the 1950 census. Duncan (1961) then used the regression weights from the matched set of occupation titles to produce scale values for all occupations.

[5]The Hollingshead Index of Social Position is a multidimensional scale that takes into account residence, occupation, and education. According to Hauser, it has been widely used in epidemiological research despite its extraordinarily weak empirical basis. The Nam-Powers Index is a purely relational index and a more credible competitor to the Duncan SEI, according to Hauser. It is an average of percentile standing in census income and education distributions.

which women are a very important component of the labor force. In addition, it turns out that education alone generates a better scale than composite indexes, such as those that include both income and education. The story of the Duncan SEI is a case history of the rise and fall of a standard sociological measure that became obsolete over time. There is now an international socioeconomic index developed by Treiman and colleagues that is well suited for comparative work.[6]

Normalization of Metrics

Multiplicative scales and log transformations are analytic schemes for normalizing metrics to achieve comparability in levels or effects. Hauser discussed how such transformations can range from truly useful to utterly misleading.

One of the simplest and most powerful transformations, under appropriate circumstances, is the log transformation. Because log transformations reduce positive skew and increase negative skew, it is often desirable to add a constant (start value) before transforming the original variable.

Both location and metric affect comparisons. Hauser pointed out that interaction effects may be an artifact of differences in location on the same scale (when effects are not linear). As an example, he pointed to comparisons of returns to education among blacks and whites in the United States (Hauser et al., 2000). Vignette measurement circumvents some of these problems by trying to calibrate individual scales, rather than trying to assume that there is a common scale for everyone in ordering objects (see King et al., 2004).

Hauser turned next to meta-analysis, which typically involves statistical analyses of the combined results from different analytic studies. In his view, meta-analysis is vastly inferior to pooled analyses of primary data. In particular, the dominant use of "effect size" in standard deviation units does not create common understanding, since these units are not necessarily in the same metric and are not real units. As data sharing increases and as people's capabilities to use multiple sources of data increase, his hope is that meta-analysis will become less important.

Hauser's selective review of past efforts provides a cautionary account of the prospects for useful and valid common metrics in the social sciences. He ended his presentation with seven lessons for the creation of sound, standard, and comparable social, economic, and behavioral measures:

---

[6]See Ganzeboom, De Graaf, and Treiman (1992) for discussion about the International Socioeconomic Index of Occupational Status.

1. Repeated use gives meaning to a metric; overuse may reify it.
2. Meet a real scientific and/or policy need. If no one else will use a measure, it is not worth the effort. Widespread use is rewarding. A check of citation indexes attests to the fact that the biggest citation counts go to people who develop useful measures, not those who analyze data.
3. Seek simplicity in content and construction. To the extent that an indicator is hard to ascertain, is complicated to construct, and admits multiple interpretations, it will be less useful.
4. Avoid relative measurement: above all, avoid percentile ranks, standard deviations, and shares of variance.
5. Avoid descriptive terms for arbitrarily or subjectively determined ranges of a quantitative indicator. Such terms invite misinterpretation.
6. Study the operational and analytical behavior of a measure to assess its validity, not merely the details of its construction.
7. Weigh the balance between internal and external validity. Information loss may vary positively with comparability, and sometimes loss is gain.

His closing remark was that nothing is more important and scientifically rewarding than the development of standard metrics that are useful in theory and in practice.

DISCUSSION

In her discussant remarks, Christine Bachrach (Duke University and University of Maryland) posed three broad questions to further extend the range of issues based on her reading of the workshop papers and presentations.

First, how healthy is measurement science in the social sciences? Understanding common metrics to advance social science theory as the focus of the workshop, Bachrach probed whether theory is actually advancing metrics, common or not, in an adequate fashion in the social sciences. It is important to carefully define the constructs one wants to measure, she cautioned.

In addition, Bachrach noted that the seriousness with which measurement is approached and the degree to which it is grounded in scientific principles and scientific methods actually vary tremendously across the behavioral and social sciences. She observed that there are structural factors that contribute to placing measurement on the sidelines, chief among them the balkanization of disciplines, with some placing greater emphasis on measurement issues.

In the field of demography, the use of common measures is fairly well accepted in the design and development of omnibus surveys. Although this has many positive benefits, Bachrach noted that it also leads to the development of "habitual measurement practices," that is, relying on the same measures regardless of whether they truly represent the theoretical constructs of interest. For example, years of schooling are measured quite similarly across the social sciences, although the measure is used to operationalize very different theoretical constructs ranging from opportunity cost to human capital to social class. She echoed a point made by Hauser about users reading into measures what they want. Thus, common measures alone are insufficient if there is a lack of common understanding as to what those measures represent. She identified the structure of peer review as yet another set of factors that influences the health of measurement science in the social sciences. NIH has recently shifted its review criteria to try to nudge reviewers away from a very detailed focus on the technical approach used in grant applications to a focus on impact, significance, and innovation. There always has been tremendous variation across different review groups as to how much attention is given to the quality of measurement and the approach taken to measurement; she supposed that this new change may further dampen attention to measurement. Bachrach saw similar variations in the peer review of journal articles in terms of the importance accorded to measurement issues.

Second, what is meant by common metrics? Bachrach encountered multiple meanings in her reading of the workshop papers. The workshop planners describe common metrics in terms of researchers who are pursuing a line of inquiry that relies on common measures for the variables under study. Some people mean the development of standard measures that are driven by policy needs and institutional requirements (e.g., poverty, race, high school completion). Hauser referred to these as public metrics, but said that through their use in policy they may take on a life of their own. Another meaning suggests the development of methods for aligning different measures with each other, as illustrated by international benchmarking of educational measures and approaches to normalizing and transforming metrics to achieve better comparability. Yet another meaning that is less explicit is associated with the idea that investigators situate their measures with respect to others in play.

Although the focus of the workshop is on social science theory, Bachrach observed, the papers are more concerned with the needs of policy. She cautioned that how one goes about developing common metrics for advancing policy may differ from the approach recommended for advancing theory. Even the definitions captured in the workshop description cover a very broad set of scenarios depending on how a line of investigation is interpreted. In her view, perhaps the best contribution that this workshop could make would be to map out the very different forms that pursuing common metrics can take, depending on the state of the science and the goals in play. She also said that it would be worthwhile for the workshop to address how the different forms fit together and whether there are cases in which insufficient attention to the value of common metrics is holding back science.

Third, how does the social science community move from the successes of the past to tackling new opportunities and challenges? She noted two examples of metrics that have stood the test of time through very careful, thoughtful revision. One is the definition of the meter, which was adopted in 1791 and grounded in the physical sciences. The measure was revised at least four times, and these revisions were driven by changes in the science used to translate the definition of a meter into an actual metric. Another example is the Duncan socioeconomic index, a measure that has been extremely successful in advancing research on social mobility. It, too, has required adaptation because of changes in the occupational structure itself and because of changes in the labor force. Bachrach suggested that there is the opportunity for developing flexible common measurement strategies that can better keep up with the diversity of experience over time and accommodate the diversity of experience that exists at any one point in time. She asked whether there might be a way to tap into new technologies, new scientific advances, to develop adaptive models of measurement that can be widely used.

At NIH, Bachrach saw many instances of disciplinary divides obstructing the flow of knowledge about constructs and appropriate measurement between the health sciences and the social sciences. She considered the balkanization of disciplines as weakening links between science and measurement because the development of measures used in one discipline may benefit from science in another discipline. Thus, the movement toward interdisciplinary research promises greater commonality of measurement. She believes there has been progress in bridging these divides.

Robert Pollak (Washington University, St. Louis, Missouri) picked up on a different sort of disciplinary divide by distinguishing between measurement reports for their own sake and measurement for use in analysis. In the latter case, he said, people ought to think about what the independent variables and the dependent variable are. For example, with respect to outcomes for children, one might be thinking about health or education outcomes (e.g., highest grade completed, test scores), labor market outcomes, or crime. He also cautioned that seemingly simple variables (such as marital status) actually can be very complex. It has become conventional practice to combine those who are cohabiting with those who are married, for example. But Pollak raised additional questions, such as how one should think about married couples who are not living together or who commute.

He recognized that these are empirical questions and not ones that can be settled easily.

Nancy Cartwright (University of California, San Diego, and London School of Economics and Political Science) emphasized the need to consider sociology and politics not only outside the academic community but also within it. She observed that there can be pressure in the academic community to use the measures of one's supervisor or to pursue the kind of results that are likely to bring professional rewards.

Harris Cooper (Duke University) turned the discussion to meta-analyses, contending that a more modern view of meta-analyses sees them as not providing definitive answers but perhaps setting the stage for where one should look to define the next experiment or investigation. He acknowledged that meta-analyses can only be as good as the studies that are included in them. He sees his colleagues in medicine as leading the way with regard to use of what they refer to as individual patient data meta-analyses. Hauser responded that he sees the challenge as going from effect sizes in different studies to metrics that have more meaning. He is convinced of the need for overlapping metrics in different studies in order to get to a real metric in the course of analysis.

WHAT CAN BE LEARNED FROM THE ECONOMIC SCIENCES?

Robert Willis (University of Michigan) provided some history on standardization, touching on the politics associated with standardizing measures in economics before turning attention to the U.S. national accounts. National accounts represent a standardization of method and approach that has been quite powerful yet incomplete in a fundamental way. There are ways to make them more complete by essentially using extensions of standard methodology, such as gathering better data and developing better theory. Willis discussed another approach, which is to complement so-called objective measures with more subjective ones. He also argued that established statistical agencies have had to apply economic theory in order to produce economic data that are useful and credible for science and for policy.

Historical and Political Considerations

Willis began by observing that because economics is so directly relevant to policy and politics in a democratic society, the development of standardized economic data has gone hand in hand with the development of the idea of data in public service. He recounted the history of the formation of the National Bureau of Economic Research (NBER) to illustrate the tradition in the field of connecting facts (data) and policy. Founded in 1920 as a private institution, the NBER charter incorporates appreciation for the explicit connection between facts and policy, emphasis on scientific principles and impartiality, and the expectation that the bureau should abstain from making recommendations on policy (Fabricant, 1984).

As recounted by Willis, the first NBER project can be considered a case study of professionalization in the production of standard measures. National income measurement is based on a close connection between economic theory and the definition of the measurement tasks. In the 1930s, the project moved to the newly formed Bureau of Economic Analysis (BEA) in the U.S. Department of Commerce, national income accounts became part of the official statistics of the United States, and the methodology was adopted by other countries around the world. Willis noted the explicit attempt, first in the founding of the NBER itself and later in the incorporation of this work into the government, to make the production of the data as resistant as possible to political and other pressures.

In addition to BEA, Willis counted the Census Bureau, the Bureau of Labor Statistics, and others as federal statistical agencies committed to the collection of objective data free of partisanship and advocacy. He recalled various crises in which professionals in statistical agencies have stood their ground, refusing to manipulate a measure, such as the unemployment rate, for political advantage. A case in point can be seen in the advice given by Francis Walker—the superintendent of the 1870 census, the founding commissioner of the Bureau of Labor Statistics, the inaugural president of the American Economic Association, and a vice president of the National Academy of Sciences—to the first commissioner of the Massachusetts Bureau of Labor Statistics (Walker, 1877: vii-viii as cited in Prewitt, 1987):

> Your office has only to prove itself superior to partisan dictation and to the seductions of theory, in order to command the cordial support of the press and the body of citizens. . . . I have strong hopes that you will distinctively and decisively disconnect [the bureau] from politics.

Measurement in Economic Life

In elaborating on the connection between theory and policy, Willis turned next to measurement in economic life. People enter exchanges only if they believe they are getting more than they give. Just as standardized measurement of physical quantities and monetary values have ancient origins (see Bohrnstedt, 2010), so do the actions of private actors and sovereigns to subvert the standards, or capitalize on asymmetric information, for their own advantage.

Willis pointed to measurement of gross domestic product (GDP) as the canonical example of standardized measurement in economics. GDP is reported by BEA in the United States and similar agencies throughout the world. The basis for these aggregate measures lies in micro-level surveys of households, firms, and units of government, as well as administrative records. The measure is intended to allow comparisons of real income levels in a given country across time and across countries at a given time. To make the comparisons, adjustments must be made for differences in the purchasing power of a monetary unit using price indices.[7]

Another of the NBER's projects concerns business cycles, work that is empirical and atheoretical, motivated by the idea that one needs to gather an abundance of facts to understand business cycles. In 1947, Tjalling Koopman made a very strong argument that measurement should be guided by theory, and economists by and large have abided by this ever since, with a standard set of beliefs in common practice.

Willis outlined a number of assumptions that have been very important in the history of economic thought, all of which are quite innocuous on their own. These assumptions include utility-maximizing consumers and profit-maximizing firms in a perfectly competitive market economy, with all quantities and prices being observable. He noted the scientific contribution of measures of price, quantity, and income as follows:

- Income and related variables are cardinal measures that can be added, subtracted, multiplied, divided, logged, and exponentiated.
- At the micro level, these variables are the outcomes and determinants of the behavior of individuals and firms that economic science seeks to explain.
- At the macro level, short-run macroeconomics and long-run studies of economic growth depend on consistent measurement of aggregate quantities over time.
- Real income and related measures provide meaningful, interpersonally and intertemporally comparable measures of welfare that can be compared across subgroups.

Willis elaborated on the idea that real income, which is income adjusted for inflation, can be used for economic welfare analyses that are relevant to policy often without knowing very much about individual characteristics or preferences. In discussing data demands for welfare analyses, Willis explained that the method of revealed preferences requires knowledge of the full choice set. An individual's choice set is determined by his or her income derived from the ownership of resources and the market price of the goods and services available. He noted that data on goods and services consumed

---

[7]Purchasing power parity indices are embodied in the Penn World Tables, a major effort that allows conversion of incomes in different countries to comparable measures (Deaton and Heston, 2010).

and market prices omit much of what goes into people's preferences. For example, public goods provided by the government enter into the national accounts at cost, since there is no way of valuing them. The environment is a nonmarketed shared resource, nothing of which appears in the national accounts. Individual consumption in families and households, as well as future (or lifetime) consumption based on a set of expectations under states of uncertainty, also are not directly measured. When markets are absent, there is little alternative but to try direct measurement of "output."

Willis related a frustrating tale told by Angus Deaton at Princeton University about a largely failed attempt to determine trends in the number or proportion of people living on less than $1 per day. He used the purchasing power parity (PPP) approach to develop a measure of the amount of local currency needed to buy $1 worth of goods in countries around the world. Extreme poverty measured in this way is how many people live on $1 a day or less. Deaton could not get sensible results until he incorporated measures of self-rated well-being from a Gallup poll. He traced the problem with PPP to a failure to have data on prices on comparable items, such as the quality of shirts in Kenya, New York, and London. Willis interpreted Deaton's experience to reflect not so much the inadequacy of mainstream theory as the difficulty of measuring the variables demanded by the theory.

He turned next to recent development of measurements that fall outside the conventional accounting framework used in economics. He observed that economists are increasingly willing to consider supplementing their market-based measures with subjective ones. Health is a good example for which objective measures are hard to come by, and it is not clear if self-reported measures of health are valid and interpersonally comparable. Anchoring vignettes can be a way to try to disentangle the rating scale from "true" value (see Hauser, 2010).

Willis ended with his belief that economics has developed a powerful method for using market data prices and quantities to create standardized measures of income and related variables that can be compared across people, countries, and time. They can be aggregated and disaggregated by the economic framework, but the framework fails to account well for goods and services that are produced and consumed outside markets. One approach to deal with this is to develop new measures of choice sets and behavior in implicit markets. Another is to relax the economist's preference for objective data and revealed preference in favor of subjective measures. He sees very few measures based on implicit markets or subjective measurement ready for standardization in the sense of official statistics. There is great value, he said, in having comparable measures available for research that will allow improvement of new measures. Meanwhile, one needs to recognize the dangers of using imperfect or incomplete standardized measures as guides to policy.

MEASURING HEALTH-RELATED QUALITY OF LIFE

Dennis Fryback (University of Wisconsin, Madison) introduced a typology for health measures and then focused on the need for standardized "health-related quality of life" (HRQoL) indexes.

In his basic typology of health measures, Fryback distinguished between mortality-based and morbidity-based measures. Mortality-based measures are among the easiest to ascertain—life expectancies, whether someone is alive or dead. Morbidity measures and nonfatal outcomes are more difficult to track. The health field tends to rely on morbidity indicators that are usually countable (e.g., tuberculosis rate, Caesarian section rate, percentage of the population that exercises). He briefly reviewed examples of morbidity-based indicators, including Healthy People 2010, the Core Health Indicators of the World Health Organization (WHO), America's Health Rankings, and the Wisconsin County Health Rankings. Many of these measures either contain too many indicators for a useful overall assessment of progress (e.g., Healthy People 2010, WHO) or arbitrarily sum several indicators to get rankings of states to stimulate policy. Fryback argued for less arbitrary ways of summarization.

One level up are summary health status measures that proxy point-in-time summaries of a person's health, but with respect to a particular disease or organ. They are sensitive to changes in symptoms or functional impairment due to a particular disease process. Examples include the Arthritis Impact Measurement System (AIMS), the Vision Function Questionnaire, the McGill Pain Questionnaire, and the New York Heart Association Classification.

There are also generic health status measures that aim to obtain a full-spectrum profile of an individual's health. These use a relatively brief questionnaire that touches on all of the major domains of health (or at least the relatively agreed-on ones) and is not tied to just one disease or organ system. These are useful particularly in measuring the health of people who have multiple disease conditions. The ubiquitous measure throughout the world is perhaps the SF-36 health profile, Fryback said. Its 36 questions cover 8 domains of health,[8] with separate scores generated for each of two subscales: the physical component and the mental component.

Of all the generic health status indexes, Fryback favors the HRQoL to represent the overall health of the individual. The scale or score is neither a simple, psychometric sum of items nor a sum of responses to items on a questionnaire. Instead, it reflects preferences for different aspects of health, with 1 = perfect health and 0 = dead. Econometric methods are used to

---

[8]The eight domains included in the SF-36 are physical function, role functioning as affected by physical abilities, bodily pain, general health, vitality, social functioning, role functioning as affected by emotional health, and mental health.

elicit utility weights (preferences) for health states, with average preference weights from a community sample of people. He acknowledged that defining perfect health can be a problem.

Fryback returned to the two areas of concern as health outcomes—morbidity and mortality. Morbidity is how people feel, how health problems affect them, abilities, disabilities, functional capacity, independence, and other aspects of health and well-being. Mortality is how long people live. Health care and health interventions affect both of these aspects of health.

According to Fryback, one summary measure, HRQoL, combines all the aspects of morbidity. A second summary measure, quality-adjusted life expectancy (QALE), combines HRQoL and mortality into a single number. QALE would be the expected number of quality-adjusted life years (QALYs) experienced by a cohort of the same starting age and quality of life. It is perhaps the best estimate of future health-adjusted life years for a random member of that cohort.

Fryback shared other uses of QALYs. Canada follows HRQoL over time with a large longitudinal panel data as well as with successive cross-sectional population surveys. The U.S. Panel on Cost-Effectiveness in Health and Medicine tried to standardize cost-effectiveness analyses (CEA), calling for something like QALYs as the generic outcome measure for meaningful analysis. Fryback considered CEA to be more prominent in the United Kingdom and Great Britain, where the National Institute for Clinical Excellence uses QALYs as a basis for policy on what gets into the National Health Service, particularly for drug therapies.

Fryback described how cross-sectional samples of individuals' HRQoL at a point in time can be used for meaningful population health measures. Community averages of HRQoL summarize health at a point in time. Cross-sectional HRQoL data can be combined with mortality data, and life table techniques can be used to weight life expectancy computations (Molla et al., 2001). To illustrate this, he presented data on women in the United States from the 2000 census and the National Health Interview Survey (NHIS). The life expectancy for women ages 55 to 59 at that time was 27.1 years, but the QALE was 20.5 years, about a 25 percent difference. For women 10 years older, ages 65 to 69 at that time, the QALE was 13.8 years, which means that for the cohort between ages 55 and 65, the expected QALY at that time was about 6.7 years (or 20.5 less 13.8 years). It would have been 10 years had the quality of life not degraded during this period.

According to Fryback, the key to making meaningful comparisons over time and across populations is the systematic collection of standardized measures with sufficient sample sizes. To date in the United States, only a few data sets have suitable measures, and only one has committed to longitudinal data collection. He argued that the population data system should facilitate computing QALE over time. This would allow population tracking and measuring improvement in both survival and HRQoL over time. He noted that there are several potential HRQoL indexes available today that have been developed over the past 40 years,[9] each with an associated questionnaire varying from 5 to nearly 60 questions, with varying times to completion from 2 to 15 minutes on average. All of these indexes conceive of HRQoL as multidimensional, generally capturing physical, mental, and social functions, as well as experience and feelings vis-à-vis some important symptoms (e.g., pain, anxiety, depression). They all attempt to locate the individual in a multidimensional health space; that multidimensional health state is then scored by some sort of preference-based weighting function based on population data.

The HRQoL indexes all differ. They use different dimensions, or they conceptualize dimensions differently. They rely mostly on Guttman scales or Likert scales to describe dimensions, but they use different categories, different levels, and different numbers of categories. Their scoring functions are based on utility assessments made by people sampled from the populations, but different populations and different econometric methods to elicit these preferences are used. As a result, the indexes are related but different, and each has flaws (e.g., differential coverage and differential sensitivity among health domains, ceiling and floor effects), which may explain why the United States has not adopted a standard HRQoL measure. Perhaps the most contentious issue among the different indexes is where they place the dead. Three of the scales have health states worse than dead.

In an effort to assess the different indexes and how they relate to a common underlying latent scale of health, Fryback et al. (2010) used item response theory in a novel way to put six of them on a common scale and compare them. Two appeared linearly related, but the others showed ceiling effects and therefore were not linearly related. The authors concluded that these indexes are clearly not identical and are imprecisely correlated.

Fryback identified a number of other barriers to adopting a standard HRQoL index for U.S. surveys:

- Competing developers and proprietary interests, which discourage U.S. agencies from endorsing a measure that would create a financial winner and losers.
- The perceived large incremental response burden to add an entire HRQoL questionnaire onto a national survey, when it can be challenging to add even one or two questions.

---

[9]The indexes include the Quality of Well-Being scale, Self-Administered (QWB-SA), the Health Utilities Indexes, the EuroQoL EQ-5D, the SF-6D, and the Health Activities and Limitations Index (HALex).

- U.S. aversion to using weights from other countries.
- Lack of interest from NIH institutes that are generally disease- or organ-focused and seek measures sensitive to their issues, with the National Institute on Aging being the exception.

Patient-Reported Outcomes Measurement Information System

PROMIS is part of the NIH Roadmap using IRT to scale the different domains of health. Each dimension has its own item bank and scale, which can be improved over time. Fryback described the conceptual framework for health in PROMIS as similar to HRQoL, but the measurement basis is very different. In PROMIS, IRT is used to create a separate psychometric scale for each dimension; there is no combining of scales into a single summary. He reported that PROMIS has developed an Internet-based interface using computer-adaptive testing to minimize response burden. Item banks are now available for only a few of the health dimensions; once there are item banks for all of the dimensions, PROMIS can use psychometric techniques, including IRT, to scale health items, and it can be improved over time as questions are added and improved and not necessarily affixed to one questionnaire. The final step, said Fryback, is to implement a scoring function to complete the HRQoL index. He believes there are many reasons to implement standard measures of HRQoL and that PROMIS offers a path for the future.

DISCUSSION

In his remarks, Jack Triplett (Brookings Institution) discussed the role of theory in economic measurement, but balanced it with a discussion of the limitations of economic theory as a guide to economic measurement. On the measurement of medical care in economics, he tied Fryback's presentation on medical outcomes measures to problems in the economic measurement of medical care prices and output to show how some measurement problems in economics require information from outside economics.

To illustrate the usefulness of economic theory, he offered three examples of cases in which construction of economic data is guided by economic theory:

- **Gross domestic product:** The basic structure of GDP is given in the equation $Y = C + I + G$, where Y is income generated, C is consumption expenditures, I is investment expenditures, and G is government expenditure. This equation is a fundamental analytical equation that comes right out of macroeconomic theory developed by Maynard Keynes more than 70 years ago. The basic structure of macroeconomics is still built around this equation. In the national accounts literature, this equation is usually called an accounting identity, but it is properly understood from macroeconomic theory as an equilibrium condition. There is therefore a linkage between the basic macroeconomic theory, the macro structure of the accounts, and macroeconomic analysis, which is based on the theory.

- **Consumer price index:** Triplett noted that the Bureau of Labor Statistics (BLS) considers the CPI to be an approximation to a cost of living index, which is an established concept in economic theory. He added that the BLS regards the producer price index as an approximation to a different economic concept, which is based on the theory of the output price index. The BLS is therefore an example of a statistical agency producing economic series that explicitly correspond to economic theory.
- **Economic classifications:** Triplett recalled that since 1997 the United States (indeed, all of North America) has produced industry classifications that were guided by the economic theory of aggregation. An industry is an aggregation of producing units.

Triplett also offered examples of economic statistics for which no theory seems to apply. For example, he knew of no economic theory that guides the unemployment rate. Economists use it as a measure of excess supply, but there is no tight linkage between the unemployment rate and the concept of excess supply. He remarked that the questionnaire used as the basis for estimating the unemployment rate is motivated by search theory, not labor supply (that is, it asks if the respondent has looked for work, not the number of hours the respondent wants to work at existing wage rates).

As an additional limit to the application of economic theory to economic measurement, he noted that sometimes economists disagree on the interpretation of theory. In other cases, some economists may deny that a particular theory applies to an economic measurement—this has happened in some discussions of the CPI in recent years.

Triplett turned next to quality differences between goods and services that can undermine cross-country comparisons and inter-temporal comparisons. Constructing any price index or output measure must take into account gradations of quality. In medical care, quality change arises with changes in treatment. The basic unit of measurement for medical care output is a treatment for a disease. However, Triplett pointed out, the treatment can change over time. If treatments are improving, simply counting identical treatments will underestimate the growth in medical output. What is needed to adjust medical care output measures (and medical care price measures) for improved treatments is a medical outcome measure, of the type discussed by Dennis Fryback. The importance of probable mismeasurement of medical care output is highlighted by the fact that current measurement approaches result in reported negative productivity growth in the U.S. medical care industry. This is an area in which improved measurement does not depend on economic theory. What are needed are measures of medical outcomes, like those Fryback discussed. Triplett added that there are many cases in economics in which improvement of an economic measurement depends on getting information from other social and natural sciences.

In her discussion, Kathleen Cagney (University of Chicago) distilled some of the main points from Fryback's presentation and focused on challenges and opportunities related to the measurement of HRQoL. Turning attention to the three classes of HRQoL measures—generic health indices and profiles, disease-specific measures, and preference-based measures—and their interplay, Cagney considered how generic and disease-specific measures focus on the presence, absence, severity, frequency, or duration of symptoms and how these are drawn from psychometric theory, whereas the preference-based measures relevant for assessing preferences of individuals for alternative health states or outcomes are drawn from economic theory and ideas of comprehensiveness and comparability.

Cagney referred to the seminal work of Patrick and Erickson (1993), which defines HRQoL as the value assigned to duration of life as modified by impairments, functional states, perceptions, and social opportunities that are influenced by disease, injury, treatment, or policy. In contrast, the definition offered by the Centers for Disease Control and Prevention assumes that HRQoL is synonymous with health status but also encompasses reactions to coping with life circumstances.

Cagney referred also to the objectives of health status assessment as outlined by Patrick and Erickson (1993): to discriminate among persons at a single point in time, to predict some future outcome or results of a more intrusive or costly criterion measure, and to measure change over time (e.g., cohort study). Consistent with the tenor of Fryback's presentation, Cagney shared Colleen McHorney's (1999) observation that the "field of health status assessment is regarded more for how it quantifies and validates health status indicators than for how and why it conceptualizes health." Cagney considered the SF-36 a standard in health status assessment. It is responsive to 44 disease conditions, and it has been translated into more than 50 languages. However, as McHorney has pointed out, there are 8,360 different ways to score 50 on the SF-36 physical functioning scale, which is only half of the SF-36 measure. What is important in Cagney's view is to consider the progression of disease over the life course and how one shifts from the initial position of health decline to a later state of physical frailty.

Cagney summarized a number of challenges associated with the HRQoL measure. She highlighted Fryback's sense that HRQoL scores describe but do not actually value health, a goal that may be informed by the work of

PROMIS. Other challenges include difficulty agreeing on a common set of metrics and the need to create or demonstrate valid and reliable measures across population groups. There is also the challenge of assessing change that involves not only aging but also the perception of the change with age, taking into account individual abilities to adapt. Another challenge is the tension between the needs of large-scale survey enterprises and clinical settings. Measures that have emerged in a clinical setting have a different set of goals (to augment clinical decision making) than those in population surveys (to more broadly inform social science and policy), and, in that sense, they may not be robust in a larger social survey setting. Fryback also had observed that rankings seem to mobilize the American psyche. Cagney remarked on the importance of thinking about policy-related goals when using HRQoL measures.

Cagney closed with a summary of opportunities. She saw HRQoL measures as potentially providing insight into geographic variation. These measures also instill a greater appreciation for the role of subjective assessments, as Willis noted in his presentation. She endorsed the idea of potentially triangulating survey data resources with clinical assessments that come from the hospital or from a physician's office. There is also opportunity to focus on a framework for the study of cultural comparisons, to consider the larger social context and the bridging of mental and physical components, and to operationalize the social component for inclusion in social surveys. Cagney cautioned that even a very simple notion of walking across a small room, which is used as a robust indicator of disability status, is not necessarily translatable. Another opportunity is to think about HRQoL measures in concert with biomarkers. She saw an opportunity for the social sciences to improve the understanding of health, pointing again to the potential of PROMIS and other data sources to augment this understanding.

OPEN DISCUSSION

David Grusky (Stanford University) picked up on the comment that one of the major obstacles to adoption or standardization of HRQoL measures is that there is debate about whether or not to allow respondents to score some states worse than dead. According to Fryback, some measures do not allow for states worse than dead, despite the fact that there is always a small segment of the population that identifies certain conditions (such as chronic unremitting pain, inability to do self-care activities, dependence on others for toileting, dressing, etc.) as worse than dead. Pollak raised two other points that support the reality of states worse than dead: (1) in estate planning, the use of living wills and advanced directives reflect an expression of preference for death and (2) suicide suggests that there are states worse than dead.

The challenge is how to incorporate these opinions into a data set and model them mathematically in a nonarbitrary way. The analytic methods are not yet developed, and not all index developers agree that states worse than dead should be allowed. In fact, there are some who refuse to believe that such states exist. According to Fryback, the only tool available right now is to average all the different points of view. In comparing the different indexes, Fryback speculated that it is more a matter of preference in scaling rather than a substantive issue. He wondered if it would make sense to try to reach different preference subgroups with different scales.

Hauser is not convinced that it is necessary to obtain different evaluations for different population subgroups. It struck him that a good quality of life metric would need to demonstrate some invariant properties for the ratings across different populations and different segments of the same geographically defined population. Otherwise, it would be difficult to make sense of those as utilities in an aggregate analysis. Fryback pointed out that there is nothing in the theory to suggest that everyone has the same underlying set of preferences that would lead to such invariance. As there is no way to assign people to one preference or another, he saw no way around needing to ask respondents their preferences. However, he pointed out that many different HRQoL systems order the states and scale them in approximately the same way.

Paul Courtney (National Cancer Institute) expressed concern about the trade-off between an overly reductionist approach and fidelity of measurement. Fryback agreed that the tension between essentially descriptive detail and the ability to summarize aggregated higher levels with standard measures is very real for health measures. His interest has mostly been in the measures that aggregate rather than disaggregate for deep understanding of pathways to outcomes. But he pointed to the WHO aggregate measure, which includes an extensive list of environmental factors (e.g., curb cuts) that can greatly affect the quality of life for someone with restricted mobility. Fryback further believes that the social environment must be included more than it has been. This would include consideration of whether a person can interact with friends, perform a job role, engage in outside social activities, have intimacy. Fryback saw the potential for PROMIS in reinforcing the idea of standardized patient-reported outcome measures across the NIH and across the broad front of medicine.

Robert Michael (University of Chicago) directed attention to the distinction between standardization and harmonization. Harmonization has more to do with coordination, and it is often encouraged as a way to facilitate joint analyses and thus preferred to rote standardization. Willis described how harmonization has been a major issue for the Health and

Retirement Study (HRS), as it has generated comparable studies throughout Europe and Asia. He elaborated that in comparisons of indicators from more than one country, it is important that observed differences be attributable to actual differences in behavior of the people in those countries and not to differences in measurement. Hauser added occupation-based measures of social class as a positive example of harmonization, for which it is relatively easy to obtain all the information needed to produce several different measures in a single survey operation. Willis pointed to the cross-fertilization of ideas across surveys as key to driving innovation in the HRS. He favored keeping studies like it as live scientific enterprises, drawing mutual inspiration from other studies.

Bohrnstedt agreed that harmonization is one way to think about common metrics, but he did not want to neglect the fact that more effort should go into improving measurement, that is, trying to understand some latent construct and how it should best be represented.

3

Indicators

One session of the workshop was devoted to the topic of advantages and disadvantages of standardizing social science indicators. Disability indices, high school completion rates, and the construction of race and ethnicity categories were the primary examples discussed. A consistent theme was the paramount need for theory as well as a public policy purpose for motivating standardization of measurement for a particular construct.

THE STANDARDIZATION OF INDICATORS USED IN POLICY

Geoff Mulgan (The Young Foundation) described his specific perspective on the use of standardized indicators in policy making and decision making. He has experience working for several political leaders committed to using such indicators, including former prime minister Tony Blair, Australian prime minister Kevin Rudd, and the prime minister of Greece, George Papandreou, who is currently addressing a set of issues around harmonization and standardization related to national debt. He noted that, in the United Kingdom, the National Institute for Clinical Excellence is an independent, formal government body set up to determine the cost-effectiveness of different health treatments, from pharmaceuticals to smoking cessation. He is currently attempting to encourage governments to develop similar types of institutes in other fields, such as education and criminal justice in other countries.

In addressing the political context around standardization, Mulgan stated that governments in the 17th and 18th centuries tended to standardize and measure for central control (for example, tax collection), but that

approach has evolved into one of viewing standards as a tool for accountability and democracy. In addition, he observed, some of the long-run
trends involve measuring, not things, but rather less tangible concepts and
intangibles, as well as moving from single measures to indices and from
activities to outputs and outcomes. Also, there is a movement from objective facts to subjective measures of experience, for example, fear of crime
as well as crime volume, patient satisfaction, and other relational measures
of trust and feedback as well as classic health outcomes. He observed that
a broader shift to complement output and outcome measures with relationship measures is moving quickly around the world, although with less
speed in the United States. In addition, he told the audience, measurement
has moved from being primarily an issue for policy makers and the state
to becoming a source enabling the public and media to assess the progress
made by government. The latter includes measuring performance at the
local level, with indicators set at the level of very small neighborhoods as
well as the town or city.

Mulgan asserted that these new uses of indicators regarding place raise
two major issues related to experiential relational data and the balancing of
present performance and future prospects. Specifically, what is the appropriate benchmark? And how can these measures of assessment of current
performance be combined with some dynamic indicators to determine the
future success of that area, for example, in terms of individual and business
resilience?

Weaknesses and Risks in Standardization

Mulgan listed several classic weaknesses inherent in more widespread
use of metrics in policy:

- **Excess simplicity:** There is a risk of using excessively simple responses to complex problems, such as unemployment rates, that
  can distort reality or encourage excessive focus (e.g., targeting
  measures of household burglary may divert resources from other
  equally important crimes). In contrast, discussions under way in
  the United Kingdom on reducing cancer mortality focus on increasing the quality of clinical services, as well as addressing the
  environment, stress, and a host of other presumably causal factors.
- **Distortions to behavior:** There are many ways in which bureaucra-
  cies and professions respond to standardized targets, particularly
  when monetary or other incentives are involved. Examples include
  suppressing performance for fear that improvements will be used as
  baselines for impossible targets or bringing in extra resources dur-

ing periods of intense scrutiny. In general, measures that are more about outcomes than outputs are less vulnerable to distortion.

- **Diminishing utility:** For example, as soon as any measure of money supply becomes an official policy target for a government, it immediately becomes less useful because of market behavior anticipating movements in the indicator. Another example is the use of standardized tests and international benchmarking. Not only have these been powerful tools to drive up standards in mathematics and science literacy, but they also have diverted attention away from equally important but less measurable aspects of learning, such as noncognitive skills, social skills, resilience, motivation, and other key predictors of lifetime earnings, social mobility, and life success.

- **Obsolescence:** Some standardized measures reflect society or the economy at a particular point and become less useful over time. The utility for policy makers of evolving indicators may outweigh the utility of consistency.

- **Limited relevance:** While standard measurements may reflect the views of officials and professionals, they may be very different from those used by the public. For example, quality in health care services may be measured by official statistics in terms of waiting times or mortality, but the public may describe such factors as service style as most important.

Categories of Standardized Measurement: Underlying Causes and Relationship

Mulgan commented that, in most areas of public policy, there is little agreement about the fundamentals of causation and theory. Grade retention in school in the United States, for example, can be explained by economists as an issue of economic incentives of the labor market. Sociologists will insist that peer pressure is a key factor. Educators will claim that performance at age 11 affects a student at age 14, and psychologists may focus on personality structure. Consequently, he said, policy makers may not agree on which causal mode is correct, and there is no single approach to resolving disagreements.

In addition, he continued, there are also fields in which new indicators are needed, for example, the use of the Internet for public services. Related to this topic, Mulgan reported on a review that he recently conducted on the state of knowledge about behavior change and its relevance to health policy. He found an uneven evidence base on the efficacy of either financial incentives or "nudge-type" methods of environmental shaping of behavior.

Disaggregation and Aggregation

Mulgan acknowledged the difficulty in using any kind of aggregate indicators or aggregate population measures; at the same time, the key to measuring behavior change in any field rests in large part on knowing how to disaggregate or segment the population. For example, a practitioner may consider interventions to reduce recidivism among prisoners or to reduce obesity by assuming that particular interventions will be highly effective for perhaps 10 or 20 percent of the population, if selection of participants is made by cognitive style, culture, etc. However, the intervention will probably be ineffective if an entire population group is selected without segmentation. At the same time, the segmentation tools used in health services, which are based on commercial marketing, are unproven and often dismissed, he observed. According to Mulgan, there is a greater need for targeting and segmentation, yet national statistical officers, academies of science, and other similar organizations seem to want to discourage development of robust segmentation tools.

Measurements of Well-Being and Psychological Need

Mulgan identified as a major research concern in the United Kingdom the failure of many of the current measures of poverty to capture actual need. He explained that the earlier focus on material needs (e.g., money, housing, nutrition) do not cover such factors as psychological well-being, the strength of social relationships, and the like. More specifically, a person who is isolated yet reasonably materially well off may be more in need than a person who is materially poor but has very strong family support. He reported that the Young Foundation has been investigating, both through statistical analyses and case studies, ways to understand the dynamics of need in a contemporary society, giving equal weight to material, psychological, and psychosocial measures.

While psychological measures are not as well-developed as material ones, Mulgan noted, these are needed to measure well-being, life satisfaction, and other factors, such as social connectedness. He emphasized the strong impact of cultural norms in terms of how people present their levels of well-being.

Valuing Social Impact

According to Mulgan, it is important to measure social value by creating standardized metrics or tools to compare investments in programs. While the question of measuring social value has been alive in the world of policy since before the mid-1960s, he noted that there have been several waves of effort to define usable indicators. However, none has succeeded in defining anything remotely as widely accepted as GDP.[1] Mulgan offered several reasons why these methods have not been used to guide decision making, from the very nature of social science, which involves many variables, to the difficulties of allocating value, to issues with competing values. For example, economic analysis of the social benefits of not sending someone to prison conflicts with the public's view that punishment has intrinsic virtue. In this case, a conceptual clash cannot be resolved by analysis. Mulgan also believes that time horizons, used in standard commercial discount rates, are often very inappropriate for valuing social and environmental goods.

Mulgan reported that the Young Foundation has been commissioned by the British Health Service to develop a set of tools for measuring social value and the value of health service innovations, as part of a broader effort to try to guide public services to think about the long-term productivity of specific interventions. This method attempts to gather together in a reasonably consistent framework, not a single metric, but elements that are incommensurable. The process involves a consistent way of weighting everything from quality-adjusted life years and patient satisfaction, to the cost-effectiveness of different treatments, to the benefits for other public-sector bodies, like municipalities, as well as the assessment of practical implementation tools. Standardization tools are needed to compare investments in different types of activity, he observed. They are also critical to apply in the United States and the United Kingdom, where, in the next four or five years, the dominant public policy issue will be related to dramatic cuts in public spending—up to 10 or 20 percent in the United Kingdom, he said. This type of priority is forcing more attention to productivity in public services and in the private sector. He reiterated that the use of cost-based measures in GDP for public services is "completely ridiculous" and actually discredits the GDP measures themselves as well as the public-sector measures.

Mulgan summarized his major points as follows:

- There are definite benefits to standardization of some metrics applied to public policy today.
- In the context of democratic politics, there is a drive to humanize data to make measures better fit human experience, including

---

[1]Tools used to standardize and synthesize complex types of social value include cost-benefit analysis, stated preference and revealed preference methods (that draw on economics), social return on investments, quality-adjusted life years and disability-adjusted life years, and patient-reported outcome measures. Mulgan acknowledged that few of these are actually used to shape decision making in the public or nonprofit sectors.

addressing issues like relationships. The latter may not be very important to policy makers, scientists, or academics, but in fact is becoming very significant in the day-to-day practice of public services.

- Indicators are essentially feedback systems to guide decision making in public policy, but there is a risk to linking indicators too closely to policy decisions. Social science needs consistent and comparable time-series data, whereas the needs of government are more variable.
- A judgment about indicators needs to address both their construction and their use. Are they used to constrain fluid actions and decision making by governments and to assist competitive actions? Are they assisting effective judgment on conditions of considerable uncertainty and fuzzy data?
- Both data and the institutions to use them are needed. Having authoritative public bodies make judgments using standardized metrics in transparent ways is as important as having the metrics themselves, and just as important as the recognition that all of these have, in Mulgan's words, "limited half lives."

Mulgan ended by sharing his belief that even the best indicator will be useful for a time but will then need to replaced and updated, because that is simply the nature of social knowledge.

STANDARDIZED MEASUREMENT

In his presentation, Robert Pollak raised concerns about the premature application of standards and the notion that standardization will make for successful science, rather than the idea that successful science generates standardization. He gave a number of examples to illustrate his point. Family structure, in this example marital status, provides an excellent opportunity to explore the use of standardization, he said, posing several questions. Does marital status mean that one is legally married? Are cohabitants included? Are couples who are legally married but not living together included? Does the definition of marital status used as an independent variable affect the outcome when researchers try to predict educational outcomes, for example, whether a child will finish high school?

Taking this examination of factors and standardization further, Pollak raised the question of what it means to complete high school. In other words, should people with general educational development (or GED) credentials be treated as high school graduates? Citing work by James Heckman on labor market effects demonstrating clearly that GED is not equivalent to high school graduation, Pollak concluded that the question of what is being examined may determine what measurement standards are used.

Turning to disability measures, Pollak considered as a real barrier to progress the lack of consistency in the concept and definition of disability and in the analysis of trends in prevalence. Some clarification on what is meant by the term "disability" is needed, he said, since different definitions suggest different kinds of solutions and indicate different targets for interventions and actions. Pollak further stated that it is unclear in this case what standardization will achieve.

He observed that public perceptions would certainly be affected by the standardization of disability and that policy may even be affected. However, questions remain: What should be the basis for standardization? What should be the underlying assumptions? Should the definition of disability be more or less inclusive? In Pollak's view, whether standardized measurement would lead to better policy can be discussed only in terms of a particular standardization of measurement and a particular view of what constitutes better policy.

In economics, theory has implications for measurement, and economists regard measurement without theory with skepticism (Koopmans, 1947). Pollak used the example of the consumer price index (CPI) and the cost of living index to examine the use of standardized measurements for disability. The crucial aspect of having a theory is that it provided a way of dealing with a lot of hard problems that arose in constructing the CPI. The underlying theory provides a framework to refer to when questions arise that challenge the components of the index. Pollak posed the question: What counts as an argument if there is no theory to appeal to? Without a theory, he asserted, anything is equally as good as a treatment of a difficult problem. He further stated that another main advantage of theory is that it depoliticizes some of the serious choices that do have impacts on the behavior of the index.

Turning to the issue of how disability is perceived, Pollak divided the literature into three sections: (1) disability among children, (2) disability among working-age adults, and (3) disability among the elderly. Using the example of activities of daily living (ADLs), such as transferring, dressing, bathing, toileting, eating, and walking across a room, Pollak proposed that if individuals or their proxies were asked which activities pose difficulties, an index could be derived by adding up the number of positive responses. However, the questions of how the items in this index were chosen and how their weight was determined are significant. For example, does the standard list of ADLs give too little weight to cognitive impairment relative to mobility impairment? How is it determined if a new item needs to be added to the ADL list and, if it is, what weight is it assigned? Pollak argued that there is no possible response to this kind of question without an underlying model and theory.

Continuing in the context of disability, Pollak delineated three possible models or theoretical constructs. One model, which he attributed to Dennis Fryback, is an appeal to utility that attempts to identify what people actually value. Another method entails using the theory of disability to predict the probability of nursing home entry within the next year, on which an index of disability could be based. His final example was an index that predicted the medical costs associated with an individual over his or her lifetime. All of these approaches are different and imply different weights, items, and methods of calculating disability. Pollak reiterated that, without an accepted theoretical framework, there is no touchstone for resolving any of the practical problems that arise in index construction.

Pollak emphasized that his focus is on nontrivial standardization, for which the measurement choices are really about choosing what is important, commenting that this is essentially a scientific question. With nontrivial standardization, the choices between measurement protocols convey different information. In his view, measurement without theory often means measurement using implicit theory. Implicit theory is better when made explicit, so it can be openly debated. He ended by saying that science is better done in the open.

Nancy Cartwright expanded on Pollak's presentation by delineating three separate avenues by which theory contributes to measurement. The first she described as "coming up with the representation" using "heavy theory," with a lot of assumptions in the theory that are very well worked out, along with a measure that gives an upper and a lower bound in constructing the particular index. A second way is using theory, or at least empirical regularities that connect the intended quantity with the actual procedures employed in carrying out measurement. This is done to ensure that those procedures are measuring the intended concept, especially when a quantity is measured indirectly via the components of an index, and even more especially when the components of this index are aggregated into a single number. The third way is distinguishing among different concepts going under the same name across a variety of theories. Proper precise scientific definition and explicit procedures are required when the emphasis is on making predictions about future behavior or forecasting the effect of policies. Different studies serving different purposes prescribe different definitions and procedures, yet they often use the same word. It is important to keep clear which of these more exact concepts is causally connected with the outcomes of interest.

Mulgan proposed that, in addition to a different theoretical foundation of a construct, it is important to consider the existence of different philosophical lenses. For example, he delineated three perspectives related to disability: a disability rights' perspective, a public value view, and a fiscal or bureaucratic viewpoint.

Robert Willis concurred with Pollak that theory is in some sense a stabilizing influence on the nature of the measure. However, he thought the issue of invariance, an old philosophical and scientific issue, has unclear implications in an economic and social context.

Robert Hauser contested the analysis provided by Pollak and Mulgan that assumes the necessity of choosing a criterion with respect to an array of measures like ADLs. He referred to the Multiple Indicator Multiple Indicator Cause (MIMIC) model presented by George Bohrnstedt, observing that if the data are benign, a criterion may not have to be chosen.

Bohrnstedt pointed out that such outcomes as nursing home, medical, and home care costs have been the focus of the discussion. There are also costs associated with disability status with respect to income or reduced income, and these factors may all comport with the same metric, which helps in weighting on the indicator side what is making a difference.

Pollak reiterated that although there are different ways to build a framework for constructing an index, the main point is to choose one and to factor in the possibility of biases.

HIGH SCHOOL COMPLETION RATES

In his presentation, John Robert Warren (University of Minnesota) considered indicators related to the measurement of high school completion. Because of the important reasons for completing high school (economic, social, political, personal, and academic), he argued that it is imperative to develop accurate and meaningful measures of the rate at which people complete or drop out of high school. While many people assume that it should be easy to quantify high school dropout or completion rates, Warren described the confusion associated with the actual estimates. Not only are there data discrepancies between surveys, but there are also inconsistencies between the data on high school completion and the data on dropouts. He outlined three reasons why the widely used measures of high school completion and dropouts differ so much from one another: (1) different objectives and purposes, (2) technical differences in measures, and (3) differences in the accuracy of the data.

Different Objectives

In Warren's view, the biggest step that could be taken toward clarifying understanding of high school dropout or completion rates in the United States is to be consistently clear and forthcoming about why they are measured in the first place. An important reason why estimates for dropout and completion rates differ so much from one another is that they differ with respect to what they are trying to accomplish.

Economists or business leaders may be interested in characterizing the level of human capital in a population or in a region. For this purpose, the timing of high school completion (how long ago or at what age people completed high school) is not important. According to Warren, dropout status or completion rates computed from cross-sectional sample surveys are best suited to describing levels of human capital in a population. Because the goal is to describe the share of all individuals who have obtained a credential, it is important to use data that include people who may have gotten those credentials from any number of places: public schools, private schools, GED programs, community colleges, adult education programs, prisons, or the Internet. Administrative data alone are not sufficient for measuring the percentage of people in the population who fall into a particular status group.

Education policy makers may instead focus on quantifying school performance in evaluating schools (within a school district or against national standards) with respect to their "holding power." How well do schools move young people from the first day of high school through to successful high school completion?

Both the timing of high school completion and the manner in which students complete high school are necessary factors to consider. Schools may be deemed successful at moving young people through to completion of high school only if they grant regular high school diplomas within four years.

Researchers may be more interested in characterizing students' experiences in navigating through educational institutions, or in predicting the likelihood of dropping out, or in modeling the consequences of dropping out. These measures are designed to describe characteristics of students or groups of students rather than a school's attributes.

Technical Differences in Measures

Another reason that high school dropout and completion rates differ involves technical differences in how they are constructed. This is true even when comparing measures that are intended for the same purpose. All high school completion and dropout rates are based on a ratio with a numerator and a denominator: the numerator is the number of high school completers or dropouts, and the denominator is the number of people at risk of completing or dropping out. But even when measuring the same concept, there are frequently differences with respect to who has been counted as a completer or a dropout in the numerator and who is at risk of being in one of those statuses in the denominator.

$$\frac{\text{Number of Successes (or Failures)}}{\text{Number at Risk of Success (or Failure)}}$$

While it is easier to quantify success or failure in the numerator, Warren identified a number of scenarios that complicate measuring the denominator. For example, how should the denominator of a measure account for migration into or out of a particular geographic area? How should students who are expelled or otherwise pushed out of high school be counted in the denominator? When students transfer from one school to another, should they be counted in the first school's denominator, the second school's denominator, neither, or both?

In his overview of status rates, Warren explained that the fraction of the population that falls into a population subcategory is measured at a given point in time. For the purpose of describing amounts of human capital in a population or a geographic area, he addressed how status completion or dropout rates are imperfect. For example, in the previous presentation, Pollak described a method to treat all high school credentials as essentially equivalent; however, this is not necessarily the best approach, because economists have long questioned the relative labor market value of GEDs, and little is known about alternative credentials.

To measure a school's holding power, dropout and completion rates need to directly and accurately reflect a specific location. This involves the use of cohort rates, which measure the fraction of individuals who transition into a particular status among those who share a common status at the outset. Cohort rates are based on longitudinal administrative data that school districts and states keep about students. School districts are increasingly using longitudinal tracking systems to follow students over time; however, there are still problems with the way states and districts define numerators and denominators in order to lower their dropout rates. Warren argued that the most effective data would represent each graduating or incoming student cohort and be made available annually.

He discussed how few trend analyses have been completed, because measures change over time and cross-state or cross-district comparisons have been difficult to carry out. In this regard, the movement toward using standards that were initially proposed in 2008 by the National Governors Association and the U.S. Department of Education is a step forward. These standards include restricting the numerator to regular diploma recipients who obtain diplomas within four years and the denominator to people who are at risk of getting those diplomas and appropriately accounting for things like migration. If states consistently implement the standards laid out by the Department of Education, eventually cohort rates can be compared over time and across states.

Until consistently defined cohort rates that are comparable over time and space become regular practices, Warren observed, it is best to use aggregate cohort rates based on Common Core Data or similar data for research purposes. It is also important to account for the weaknesses and limitations of these sorts of measures and acknowledge the bias in research results. Individual-level data based on longitudinal sample surveys, like the National Education Longitudinal Study or the various longitudinal surveys administered by the National Center for Education Statistics, are best suited for describing students' progress through the secondary school system. However, these types of surveys are limiting because they are very expensive, are not conducted regularly, and suffer from problems of coverage bias and sample attrition.

Accuracy of Data

The third reason Warren outlined for the differences in high school dropout and completion rates has to do with the accuracy of the underlying data used to construct them. Even when the measures are intended to quantify the same thing and even when they agree on the technical definition of the numerator and the denominator, the estimates often differ. Another weakness with status completion and dropout rates has to do with the validity and reliability of respondents' self-reports of whether and how they completed high school.

A COMMON METRIC FOR RACE AND ETHNICITY?

In his presentation, Matthew Snipp (Stanford University) referred to race and ethnicity as a set of universal characteristics that exist over time and space. He observed that the human species relies heavily on the ability to visualize and identify difference, and some people have argued that the ability to make distinctions on the basis of race may have even been a selective advantage. More specifically, identifying people who look the same in terms of physical appearance, stature, diet, etc., may be a way to recognize those who are less likely to cause harm (or vice versa).

Snipp noted that the color coding of race, however, is something that is even more recent, beginning with the emergence of biology and the racial sciences in the late 18th and early 19th centuries. The rise of the racial sciences in the 19th century, principally ethnology and eugenics, focused heavily on the physiognomy of race. In the late 19th and early 20th centuries, people began contesting the research and thinking on race, especially the concepts of physiognomy and the notion of inherent racial hierarchies. In the mid-20th century, attention began to shift from trying to define race to categorizing types of race. Today, administrative definitions are probably most familiar, because they are based on some sort of administrative or political agenda.

Constructions of Race in America

Snipp explained that people construct race socially by taking behavioral and physical characteristics associated with human difference and agglomerating them into a set of traits that are called race or racial distinctions. Three entities are important in terms of determining what race is in America: legal definitions, the Census Bureau, and the Office of Management and Budget (OMB).

With regard to legal definitions, "white" is a default category conventionally understood to have some sort of European continental origin. Snipp explained that African Americans traditionally have been identified by the rule of hypodescent, the "one-drop rule," which has been reinforced by Supreme Court and federal court rulings. He noted that, in contrast, the rule of hyperdescent has been applied to American Indians, which requires minimum ancestry that very clearly restricts the magnitude of federal obligations. Each of the 562 tribes has its own criteria for determining who is an American Indian. While there is no history of either hypodescent or hyperdescent for Asians, Snipp mentioned that there is a history of restrictions regarding immigration and citizenship that was built into the 1882 Chinese Exclusion Act. Lately, discussion among the Latino community has centered around whether "brown" is a separate race, whether Latinos are a separate race, or whether the idea of Hispanic white makes sense for those who are of mixed indigenous and European origin, for example, many Mexicans.

Snipp observed that ever since the first census, conducted in 1790, questions about race have been asked. By the 1970s, there was an enormous amount of legislation, programs, and operations that required data about race. To facilitate comparison of race data, OMB-issued Directive No. 15 identifies the categories that federal government agencies should use for statistical collection and reporting.[2] The directive also notes that these classifications should not be interpreted as being scientific or anthropological in nature. All agencies, grantees, and contractors (with the exception of small businesses) were required to use this set of categories. The American people became used to seeing these categories and thus thinking about them in terms of race and ethnicity. The categories filtered into the social sciences and were reflected in textbooks about race and ethnicity. Snipp said that these categories became the foundation for basically everything that is known about race in this country.

---

[2]The categories included American Indian or Alaskan Native; Asian or Pacific Islander; black, not of Hispanic origin; Hispanic origin; and white, not of Hispanic origin.

In his view, the 1990 census was a turning point in racial measurement for a variety of reasons. It had a long list of categories that included legacy races, like white, black, and American Indian. Other categories, which listed nationalities, were followed by an instruction to circle one of them, causing many protests by such groups as Arabs, Taiwanese, and Native Hawaiians, who could not self-identify with the groups shown. Native Hawaiians, in particular, objected because they did not want to be included as Asians and Other Pacific Islanders. In addition, interracial family organizations protested against privileging one race over another in identifying children of biracial families. Others were exercised to learn that the Census Bureau editing procedure allocated individuals to one race category (mostly white) even if they had reported multiple categories.

In 1994 the National Research Council held a conference and published *Spotlight on Heterogeneity: The Federal Standards for Racial and Ethnic Classification* (National Research Council, 1996). OMB hearings were held around the country, and an interagency working group was formed. The Census Bureau conducted a number of tests in anticipation of revising the racial classifications. In October 1997, OMB released a revision of Directive No. 15 with two major changes: (1) a separate category for Native Hawaiians and (2) the option to report more than one race. The implementation of this new standard was slated to occur no later than January 1, 2003.

The *Spotlight* report developed eight principles for creating a racial classification, although very few of them have been honored. The most obvious shortcoming relates to the dictum that "the number of categories be of manageable size." Allowing multiple responses and using the five basic race categories yields 20 unique race categories; overlaying these categories with Hispanicity creates 40 unique categories. The 2000 census used 13 categories, resulting in 63 unique combinations, or 126 with the addition of Hispanic/non-Hispanic. Few would argue that these distinct categories constitute a manageable number. The fact that the Census Bureau has rarely published data for all 126 combinations is evidence that this system is unworkable to produce specifications for congressional redistricting, civil rights, or voting rights enforcement, for example. Other problems have resulted from these race categories:

- The inability of federal agencies to agree on which categories or subsets of categories to use for decision making.
- The need for OMB to produce a memorandum outlining a subset of categories that should receive special attention for civil rights enforcement (it resorted to the doctrine of hypodescent).
- Lack of compliance with Directive 15 by states, local governments, and other entities, thus hindering the exchange of statistical reports

among agencies and causing obstacles regarding implementing categories for different uses, including education.

- The five race categories of the original and revised versions of Directive No. 15 have been found not meaningful to a sizable number of Hispanics.

In 2007, the U.S. Department of Education issued new guidance and a simplified set of categories in which all persons identified as Hispanic, regardless of their race, are counted simply as "Hispanic." The five original single race categories of the revised version of Directive No. 15 are retained and persons reporting two or more races are categorized as "two or more races." One of the flaws of this system is that about 14 percent of the total American Indian population claim Hispanic origin, but this is not reported; Cubans and Puerto Ricans of African descent are also not identified. This system, in fact, undermines the comparability of data with data from agencies adhering to the 1997 standard, such as the Census Bureau.

Measuring Race: Outstanding Considerations

While the validity and reliability of data for race and ethnicity receive relatively little attention in the literature, Snipp observed that questions about this topic are becoming increasingly inescapable. Current thinking regarding reliability, for example, demonstrates that racial data are more fluid and dynamic than believed in the past. In addition, instability in the reporting of race, once viewed as a result of random fluctuations arising from poorly created instruments, can be systematically modeled and therefore merits further inquiry as an object of social scientific research.

In terms of validity, Snipp underscored two considerations: (1) some concordance of understanding about the meaning of race must exist between the researcher and the research subject and (2) there is no ability to determine entitlement to a particular heritage. Other challenges facing researchers include

- Ensuring content validity, including determining whether the race-specific categories under consideration are the correct ones and whether there is sufficient sample size to yield reliable estimates for smaller populations.
- Whether complex content entailed by the idea of race is comprehensively measured by one or more items on a survey questionnaire or interview schedule.
- The ability of respondents, particularly those of mixed racial heritage, to ignore instructions and choose to identify with a race that best reflects their own understanding of "race."

- Perceptions of others versus perceptions of self that are influenced by one's cognitive organization of racial identification.
- The use of indicia (characteristics used by an observer) versus criteria (formally established conditions) in determining group membership.

The ability to trace the continental origins of human DNA and to connect this information with other genetic traits yields a tempting schematic for measuring race in a way that can be standardized, measured objectively, and is invariant with respect to evolving attitudes and shifting public opinion. However, Snipp warned, genotypes do not necessarily correspond to phenotypes; phenotypic traits observable in the everyday lived experience of race may or may not correspond to the continental origins measured by genetic testing. Consequently, one may wonder about the connection between heritage and the observed human differences associated with race. In addition, although genes may have a great deal to say about the great migrations of human beings, they have little bearing on the everyday lived social experience surrounding racial differences. He commented that, although assays of genetic ancestry may be a convenient way to standardize race as a feature of biology, they are unlikely to prove a productive strategy for the social sciences attempting to capture and understand human action based on perceived and self-understood differences.

Snipp ended by noting that it would be ideal to have a tool for social science research that could capture the dynamic and reflexive nature of race and ethnicity, an instrument that would yield a standard unit of measure across time and space. However, he cautioned, there are few clues on how to devise such as instrument. He considered it more important to recognize that a useful measure for scientific inquiry depends on a clearly articulated definition or understanding of the concept under study—something currently lacking in the social sciences for the concept of race.

DISCUSSION

Kenneth Prewitt (Columbia University) commented first on Pollak's presentation, pointing out that he made a powerful and useful statement that, without theory, any indicator is weak to the point of being useless in policy making. This effect is clearly demonstrated by Pollak's juxtaposition of the CPI and the disability index. The CPI has a strong theoretical foundation, whereas the disability index does not and consequently its use inserts ambiguities into the policy process. Pollak argued that the dropout rate clearly demonstrates the straightforward nature of the relationship between theory and indices. Theory must be anchored in the policy process for the data and measures to have significant use. The primacy of purpose—for example, determining human capital labor skills in a given area for plant location or tracking students in school systems—drives how the denominator and numerator are conceptualized and the choice of methodology.

Turning next to Warren's presentation, Prewitt reinforced the point that the policy objective also drives the use of the data set. He suggested that, in terms of developing common metrics, more conversation is needed about the differences between administrative data and survey data. Survey data have the characteristic of being variable rich and case poor due to cost restrictions. Administrative data have the opposite characteristics: they are case rich and variable poor. Administrative data are not organized to give regression analyses about individual-level behavior. By examining the information systems of different national governments, the differences between administrative data and survey data become more apparent. In Europe the ratio is 85:15 administrative/survey data. In the United States, the ratio is roughly 80:20 survey/administrative data. If the indicators used are based in theory, then the theory itself has to connect to a public policy purpose that is primarily fixed by the administrative agency collecting the data. The control of the data is in fact with the administrative agency that collects it.

As an aside, Prewitt remarked that digital data will have a significant impact on the development of standardized measurements. The cost of the census in the United States is unsustainable, and this will result in a shift from its current reliance on survey data to increased use of administrative records and perhaps eventually on digital data. A digital footprint leaves enormous amounts of data and raises questions about what are proprietary data.

Prewitt then commented on Mulgan's presentation describing the evolution of the measurement system, based on the constant interaction between the quality of the science and the ways in which the data are used. He said that Mulgan tracked effectively the movement from easily measured items to more abstract concepts that include subjective well-being, social resilience, or social capital. This progression is reflected in policy discussions about the use of data and the role of the scientific community in influencing policy makers. It is important, he continued, to control measurement across the boundaries of a threshold, for example, spending more attention and money on those "above the threshold" to obtain more funding. Prewitt acknowledged that social scientists need to live with certain distortions, but at the same time, he noted, the scientific community has to build in as many protections as possible so that the system cannot be gamed, as well as to maintain transparency.

Prewitt emphasized one of Mulgan's key points about the direction of social science—the need to incorporate the constituencies affected into measurement, for example, in the creation of a new disability index. Prewitt lauded the Oregon benchmark program identified in Mulgan's presentation, which created the indices against which progress and the capability of its own government are measured. Prewitt also pointed to the global project Measuring the Progress of Societies, which is hosted by the Organisation for Economic Co-operation and Development (OECD) and run in collaboration with other international and regional partners. It is illustrative of the recognized importance of significant economic, social, and environmental indicators beyond GDP, such as measures of subjective well-being, organizational capacities, and innovation, to assess societal progress, he said. He noted that in the OECD conversation about progress, there is always a footnote that participating countries ought to define measures in their own way, thus undercutting the OECD's drive for standardization.

Turning to Snipp's presentation, Prewitt observed that the U.S. standardization of races into five categories in 1977 reflected patterns that trace to 220 years earlier, an indication of what he termed "bureaucratic inertia." He commented that the race classification system in the United States has attached itself successively to different policy regimes, from those that supported the Three-Fifths Rule (which drove American history for the first 60 years), to immigration restrictions, to affirmative action. Even in the 2010 census, he observed, the race classification is still based on historical patterns of discrimination.

Prewitt indicated that there is little theoretical basis for the race classification system in use today. He stated that it is impossible to standardize the race measure, especially cross-culturally. He noted that all the presentations in this session made the same major point about the need for theory and the need for public purpose. The latter, including the relevant measures, must be embedded in a conversation with the population, not just among statisticians.

Regarding the genomic revolution and its impact on classifications, Prewitt commented that genomic projects conducted around the world are being forced into the coding schemes of the United States—specifically, the OMB classifications. He expressed concern about current directions and "rebiologizing race." Prewitt saw the challenge as going beyond scientific standardization to focus on how such a system would be used, as well as its political and policy implications.

Barbara Schneider (Michigan State University) agreed with Prewitt about the lack of adequate research about administrative data. As more longitudinal data are being collected, she asked how these new data will be integrated into measures that have been based primarily on surveys. Prewitt commented that the big issue regarding administrative data is the potential ability to cross data sets from education with those on health and social services.

OPEN DISCUSSION

Jack Triplett commented on a point raised by both Prewitt and Snipp about controlling the denominator because it makes the data difficult for many purposes if ratios are based on different classification systems. As an example, Snipp pointed out that the U.S. Department of Education is not using the same categories as the Census Bureau, so the denominator comes from a different set of categories than the numerator.

Harris Cooper praised the quality of the papers presented, which he felt were especially valuable in relation to one another. Based on his understanding of the day's presentations, he did not consider it a problem that common social and health metrics and indices are not possible. It is not that they are impossible, responded Pollak, but rather it depends on the definition. For example, if the marriage category is defined only as being legally married and living together, then that definition can be used in any data set as an independent and dependent variable. He contended that it is better to have the raw data in order to see what independent variables are correlated with a given definition. While it is possible to define some notion and insist that it is used by everybody, this approach may not be advisable, he continued. Hauser said that aggregation, rather than data collection or measurement, is the key issue; the American Community Survey asks for national origin, and it is a completely open-ended question.

Prewitt and Snipp both expressed concern about the use of genetic markers in conjunction with racial and environmental characteristics, thinking that some lines of research should be avoided. Pollak raised a different topic concerning the benefits and limitations of self-reported race on the decennial census. On one hand, he said, it raises an interesting behavioral theory of what people report, but on the other it is also a topic for people interested in discrimination. He emphasized that there are different purposes in a social science context, and it is important to keep them in mind when considering various research questions. For this reason he is less concerned than Prewitt and Snipp about incorporating genomic issues related to medicine.

Taking issue with Prewitt's preference for administrative data that comes with associated costs, Grusky was interested in Prewitt's reaction to the view that they can have some leverage, since the data are intended for research purposes. Grusky continued by raising a point regarding Pollak's main concern that, in the absence of theory, standardized measurements would be vulnerable to political manipulation. He suggested that there may be other ways to protect against manipulation aside from theory, since the goal is to have consensus, which can be secured in other ways. He offered the examples of unemployment and official poverty measures as ones that are not defined by theory but are prevalent in usage. Setting the question of theory aside, Pollak considered the prevailing unemployment and poverty measures as part of the status quo, which is different from consensus but may indeed be the consensus.

Karen Jones (Customs and Border Protection) raised the question of how best to combine good program design with common metrics. She attended a briefing by the U.S. Government Accountability Office that addressed practical issues on conducting pure empirical research and how to mitigate its limitations by using the correct statistics to evaluate the data gathered. However, she said, there was very little emphasis on common metrics to evaluate training programs in one field, such as law enforcement. In her field, if something works in a given situation, it is often used in other situations as long as it meets the minimum criteria for good program evaluation design. She questioned how people like her can influence organizations, like OMB, that continually request adverse impact studies for training based on arbitrary racial categories.

Referring to the Health and Retirement Study, Willis returned to the issue of administrative data in connection with surveys. First, an obvious advantage is a more robust data set resulting from linking representative survey data with administrative data. Second, this pairing creates an issue regarding what agency is willing or unwilling to link the data. An agency that has no policy or policy research aspect will be less inclined to interact productively with social scientists. Willis argued for a two-way flow of information, noting that federally funded Research Data Centers that allow researchers access to restricted data have benefited from the exchange between Census Bureau personnel and academics. Prewitt said that ideally interaction between the producers of administrative data and social scientists would develop in such a way as to yield high-quality data, as well as better program administration from the resulting data.

Pollak had stated that one should think of a measure in terms of how the measure works in predicting a certain outcome. Triplett expressed concern about the concept of centering measurement in the political process. While measurement needs to be of value for analysis, in political and other contexts, the potential for political or other gaming poses a serious problem for statistical agencies. The unemployment rate serves as an interesting example; in the 1970s, it was extremely controversial. The issue was settled not by theory but in part by the work of Julius Shiskin, who launched several different versions of the unemployment rate (called U-1 through U-7) and showed that they all moved together over the business cycle.

The CPI also generated political debate during Triplett's tenure at the Bureau of Labor Statistics, and after. Many of the debates about changing the CPI focused on technical issues and how to apply the theory underlying the index. Ultimately, this specific debate did not call into question the integrity of the statistical agency. However, Triplett recalled the creation of unemployment rates for states and smaller areas, for which no reliable sample existed. He expressed skepticism about statistical programs that are generated from a political process.

The question of how to best use data collected from or generated by transactions conducted over the Internet was raised by Christine Bachrach. Are there research programs in place to evaluate the data, their use, and their cost-effectiveness? What will be the implications of these data on standardization?

Mulgan reported a dramatic change in the use of administrative data in the United States, the United Kingdom, and Australia. These governments have made commitments to make raw data available to the public as a default. This potentially transforms the relationship between administrative and survey data. For example, the Australian government runs competitions to see who can get the most cross-correlations, which would yield more case-rich data.

Mulgan cited other examples of the co-evolution of policy and science. One was the initiative in the United Kingdom to maintain a time-series database of health education and other records for children mainly at risk of poverty and social exclusion. The impetus for the initiative came from the academic community in an effort to learn more about the life course, protective factors, and risk factors, among others. The program is likely to be terminated for political reasons and concerns about human rights and privacy. Another example is the history of the unemployment rate in the United Kingdom, which has undergone a range of treatments, from political manipulation to a return to a theoretical measure of surplus labor supply. Returning to the discussion of race, Mulgan gave the example of the large Pakistani and Bangladeshi community in the United Kingdom that is calling for identity through faith, not race. This has created a challenge for the state as it tries to identify this community through a set of regressive, semibiological racial terms.

Prewitt proceeded to discuss the political implications of classification categories on surveys like the census. He used the example of how multiple races have been categorized in the decennial census. In 2000, when people were allowed to choose more than one race category, the category of "other" was not removed from the form (which had been on prior census forms to allow respondents to indicate if they were of two or more races). Even though "other" did not serve any theoretical purpose after the mark-one-or-more option was introduced in 2000, it remained on the form. Nearly half of the Hispanic population, mostly Mexican and Central Americans, used the "other" category to identify their race. After the 2000 census, the Census Bureau decided that the term was not a good measure and wanted to remove it from the form; however, a member of the House Committee on Appropriations included in the budget the provision that the

Census Bureau shall always include the word "other" if it asks any race questions.

Prewitt believes that the government must have a proper reason for asking questions of its population. Consequently, he saw the need for a connection between some kind of policy issue or possibilities and the concepts that the government is trying to measure. He further observed that the science of social measurement in the United States is most protected in statistical agencies. He argued that they care more than program agencies about data quality, continuity across time, standardization, and privacy and confidentiality. He then addressed the issues surrounding the ownership and management of digital data. While some Research Data Centers have already started thinking about the relationship between administrative and survey data, they have not yet addressed digital data. Prewitt raised concerns about the quality control of digital data being used by the U.S. Department of Homeland Security, since without public access there is no way to know how it is being maintained. He asserted that discussion is still needed about how to make sure society's information system is going to be housed in a place that is concerned with quality protection.

In the future, the way administrative records and surveys are linked will become increasingly important. Snipp cautioned that the scientific community will face a number of ethical issues, such as confidentiality and privacy concerns with respect to transactional data, survey data, and its linkages to administrative data. He mentioned that Stanford University, like a number of other institutions, has created a secure data center, but this kind of precaution is not being undertaken in the scientific community at large.

4

Social Science Constructs

The second day of the workshop began with a session on the theory of measurement and the identification and integration of three important aspects of standardization: ontology, representation, and procedures. A number of social science constructs were examined to better understand when standardization of a scientific concept makes sense. The examples illustrate a number of reasons for the lack of a standard measure: paucity of scholarly interest, balkanization of fields, sparse data, and politics. Consideration was given to rethinking incentives for researchers to work collaboratively on common measures that then improve and extend discourse.

THE THEORY OF MEASUREMENT

Norman Bradburn (National Opinion Research Center, University of Chicago) began his presentation by defining measurement as the assignment of values in a systematic and grounded way for some practical purpose. Toward this end, three aspects are paramount: (1) ontology—a definition of the quantity or category that identifies its boundaries, fixing what belongs to it and what does not; (2) representation—a metrical system that appropriately represents the quantity or category; and (3) procedures—rules for applying the metrical system to produce the measurement results. All three must mesh properly to realize useful and proper measurement.

Beginning with the issue of ontology, Bradburn distinguished between two kinds of concepts. The first are the more traditional, scientific concepts that refer to specific features, such as age, minimum wage, etc. The second are "Ballungen" concepts that sort things into categories based on a loose

53

set of criteria in which the members of the same category do not share any specific set of features but rather have what Wittgenstein referred to as "family resemblance." Such concepts are conglomerations with less precise boundaries, such as happiness, prestige, social exclusion, and the like.

Definitions depend on their purpose. Bradburn recalled Pollak's mention of disability and marital status as examples of concepts that could be defined for a scientific use in order to fit into a theory or be used to make predictions, or they could be related to policy needs or social descriptive purposes. He said that concepts can be characterized by explicit definition (e.g., formulas, such as income = consumption + savings), by implicit definition (e.g., from scientific uses or attempting axiomatic definitions), or by operational definition (e.g., IQ). The usual trade-off with respect to common metrics is between the accuracy of characterization and the purpose and breadth of applicability.

Once there is a definition, the next concern is that the representation matches the concept. Thus, concepts referring to specific features like age or income to some extent can have single-value functions that measure the values of concern. However, Ballungen concepts are often measured by indicators or indices. It is often difficult to do much more than simply count up different indicators, unless some mathematical structure can be imposed on them. Measurement procedures may combine variables with different underlying relations to other concepts (e.g., happiness and satisfaction). Bradburn observed that one of the tensions in the social sciences is that the more one refines a concept and the more precise one tries to make it, the more one may lose some of the associations and original meaning, and comparability across uses may suffer. To consider large numbers of indicators over time, one ends up reducing or weighting them. Where the weights come from is of crucial importance to the validity of the measure. Bradburn saw the need to address these issues of narrowing and redefinition if a particular set of indicators are to be used for prediction or explanation.

He turned next to two aspects of procedures. One is accuracy in terms of getting the true value of what one is trying to measure, and the other is precision or getting a narrow range of estimation. In the social sciences, researchers do not do much with instrumentation. The issue he identified is whether survey questions actually measure what one thinks they are measuring. He observed that there is no gold standard for almost all measures of concepts of interest to social scientists. However, in psychology at least, this problem was addressed years ago using the multitrait, multimethod approach—that is, using different measurement modes and different aspects of the concept to measure something in different ways, which all roughly converge on the same answer. Such empirical regularities strengthen the view that the measurement is correct, particularly if it is for scientific purposes, and they help to ensure that different procedures measure the same thing.

Cartwright and Bradburn (2010) proposed a number of general rules, including that the procedures need to be consistent with definitions of the concept and the particular representation of them. Empirical regularities are central to this. Cartwright added that procedures are a way of zeroing in on the concept to be defined. Most procedures are situation specific; many procedures zero in on the concept in different ways. In a new context, the linkage between concept and procedures may not hold.

One of the problems with Ballungen concepts is that the measurement procedures may violate the commonsense understanding of the concept. Bradburn considered unemployment to be a good example of this, because the way in which it is actually measured seems to violate the commonsense understanding of unemployment (in that it removes discouraged workers from the denominator). He emphasized that the subjective component can be very important. The meaning of "looking for work" is somewhat ambiguous, especially for youth. In the Current Population Survey, the report on youth behavior often comes from the parent, and the parent's view about whether a child is looking for a job could differ from that of the child.

Another often used measurement procedure is combining different variables and questions. Bradburn cautioned that it is important to assess whether the underlying relationship of those variables to other factors is the same. As an example, he has found the concepts of happiness and satisfaction to have different relationships with age. Yet in the literature to date, happiness and satisfaction are treated as if they are the same. In fact, they are related in different ways to underlying concepts.

Bradburn continued that the concepts with different procedures can suit different purposes. Measures of quality of life, even the ones from the Patient-Reported Outcomes Measurement Information System, are different for different purposes. Particularly with respect to policy-related indicators, the explicit values become an important part of the measures. These indicators, if adopted for a considerable time, become very difficult to change, because some groups have been advantaged by one set of procedures, without necessarily having a scientific basis for the choice. Values and value implications are hard to eliminate.

The kind of distinctions made in Cartwright and Bradburn (2010) have three major implications. First, common metrics are possible and desired if the definitions, representations, and procedures are all well specified and appropriate. Second, when concepts are used for different purposes, so that the definitions, representations, or procedures are different—or all of the above—then there will be difficulty getting to common measures. Third, many policy-related social science concepts lack a firm scientific or theoretical basis for their definition, and often their definitions depend on values.

The varying purposes for which they are used make common measures very difficult, if not impossible.

MEASURING POVERTY: THE QUESTION OF STANDARDIZATION

Robert Michael (University of Chicago) discussed the measurement of poverty in terms of the advantages and disadvantages of standardization of a scientific concept. He began by reviewing the measurement of poverty—how it is done and whether there is or is not science involved. He then reflected on lessons learned from the fact that, for the past half-century, the United States has had an officially sanctioned standardized measure of this particular construct, which forms the basis of many programs. He began by tracing five steps to measuring poverty:

1. Choose a concept of poverty. It can be a relative or an absolute concept. Science can provide guidance about the concept, but it cannot help with issues of relative or absolute. It can explain the implications but not distinguish right from wrong.
2. Select a unit of observation or analysis—individual, family, or household. The individual is probably the best unit for measuring poverty, because utility and well-being are generally individualized notions. However, individualized metrics of poverty are not conventionally seen. Most use family (connected by blood or contract) or household (everybody living under one roof and pooling resources).
3. Determine the poverty threshold level and decide how to adjust that level across units, time, and location. Acceptable equivalents across units must be determined, and this typically is based on some kind of underlying understanding of the science involved.[1] Adjustments also must be made over time. Over time, prices change, the consumption bundle underlying the notion may change, and the product and the social norms may change. Adjustments for region or location may be required if prices vary by geography.
4. Determine what resources to include. Theory or science may call for consumption as the appropriate concept to measure, but be-

---

[1]Michael described the antifamily element of the current U.S. definition of poverty. Two cohabiting people who are unrelated each have their own individual poverty threshold. If they married, the poverty threshold that would be applied to them would not be two times the one; it would be the scale equivalent level for two than one. Thus marrying would move many people near the poverty level out of poverty and make them no longer eligible for a lot of the programs they are eligible for if cohabiting and living together but treated as two separate individuals.

cause there are often too many public goods for which consumption is impossible to capture, expenditures or income are often used for practical purposes.

5. For each unit, compare the threshold to the resources and, if the threshold is higher, that unit is "in poverty," otherwise not.

Michael observed that science can provide much guidance on many but not all of these points, and it depends on the purpose of the measure. He identified three purposes for which a poverty measure is needed: (1) as a scientific measure of economic deprivation, (2) as a measure of social compassion, and (3) to determine eligibility for social programs. Standardization makes sense for the third purpose because of the importance placed on equitable treatment in eligibility. For the first two purposes, Michael does not believe that standardization necessarily makes sense.

In his view, politics and vested interests explain why it is so difficult to shift away from the use of a clearly imperfect poverty measure. Any time there is a scientific measure that translates into policy, politics will trump science, he said. Poverty is one of those issues that impacts the allocation of funds, so it is understandably of immense interest to politicians. He pointed as an example to a major National Research Council (NRC) effort that tried to uncouple the concept of poverty measurement from eligibility (National Research Council, 1995); the report, *Measuring Poverty: A New Approach*, has never gained traction, despite its being a good idea.

Michael closed by listing a number of lessons learned related to standardization:

- If the science does not suggest a consensus, it cannot impose one and expect to achieve consensus. It is not worth the effort to pursue standardization if it is not needed. One risk to unnecessary standardization is that weaknesses get codified and reinforced over time.
- Competition in general is good. Others will adopt what is seen as the better measure. For example, national income accounts have been adopted because they are a good idea. This is also true of the "earnings function" of Jacob Mincer. It too became the standard because it won the competition of ideas and because of its clarity and feasibility.
- A community of scientists who are freely cooperating powers scientific discovery. Each person, acting on his or her own initiative, acts to further the entire group's achievements (see Michael, 2010).

A NATIONAL PROTOCOL FOR MEASURING
INTERGENERATIONAL MOBILITY?

David Grusky began his presentation by observing that there is no standardized measure for intergenerational mobility largely because of the paucity of scholarly interest in standardization, the balkanization of fields, and sparse data. Much academic research on intergenerational mobility is conducted in economics and sociology, quite independently and separately from one another. Economists are focused on economic standing and economic mobility; sociologists are focused on occupations and social mobility. This balkanization of fields may be precluding the rise of a standardized measure for intergenerational mobility. Researchers have to date been more focused on the science itself and moving the academic debate within their own disciplines. In addition, he argued, the data are not available to carry out the study of mobility in any compelling way. The paucity of data has led to a "cacophony of very clever models," a situation that does not lend itself to the rise of a single standardized approach.

In each of the two disciplines, there is some amount of infighting, Grusky observed. In economics, the concept of economic standing is seen as important, but there is debate about how to operationalize it. In sociology, there is consensus on how to measure occupation, but there is debate about how best to understand occupational mobility and what it means about the social world.

In economics, the preferred method is calculating the intergenerational elasticity of income, but its calculation has been hampered by small sample sizes and measurement error. The consensus view is that there is insufficient sample size in the Panel Study of Income Dynamics and the National Longitudinal Surveys to reliably glean trends, and there are not enough repeated observations of income. These deficiencies have generated two cottage industries to provide tabular analyses of income mobility (based on quintiles) and wealth mobility.

In sociology, occupation is considered an omnibus extra-economic measure of social position, comparing, for example, the occupation of fathers with that of sons or daughters. Perhaps the most compelling argument on behalf of an occupational operationalization of mobility is that it embodies information about where an individual stands in the social world. It signals the skills and credentials (and hence life chances) of the individual, socioeconomic status and prestige, consumption practices and leisure activities, and the social and cultural milieu in which he or she lives.

Grusky considered it a potentially useful division of labor for economics to focus on economic mobility and for sociology to focus on social mobility. This permits examination of the extent to which the social worlds in which people find themselves are the same as those in which their parents find themselves. Both sociology and economics are focused on the economic standing of individuals and how it is transferred from one generation to the next. However, one could take a more narrow interpretation of occupational income as a measure of permanent income, so that the annual variations in income that one observes could be seen as noise centering on the occupational mean.

Another line of debate in sociology is about how the reproduction of social standing from one generation to the next is secured. Grusky described three types of reproduction, each with its own subtradition of analysis:

1. Gradational form—parents pass on a hierarchical position (i.e., amount of resources) associated with a particular occupation. Children of parents with many resources (social, cultural, economic) end up in good occupations; children of parents with few resources fare less well.

2. Big-class form—children inherit a big class of origin (e.g., children of professionals become professionals) with associated cultures, networks, and skills. Class-specific resources are transferred from one generation to the next, which would raise the probability of class reproduction. Two big classes of the same overall desirability (e.g., proprietors, nonmanual laborers) do not convey identical mobility chances.

3. Micro-class form—children benefit by resources or perspectives quite specific to the detailed occupations that parents might have. For example, the attack on the World Trade Center might generate family discussion about motivation and cultural differences in a family of sociologists, but discussion about structural integrity and construction materials is more likely to occur in a family of engineers.

Putting aside narrow-gauge methodological problems for now, Grusky underscored the primary need to overcome two main structural obstacles to developing a national protocol for measuring intergenerational mobility: the balkanization of economics and sociology traditions and sparse data. He sees value in maintaining both economic and sociological approaches to studying mobility. Economic position is distinct from occupation as an omnibus measure of social position. One obviously cares about how much money people have, but one also should care deeply about the social and cultural milieu in which they live and whether or not the milieu in which they grew up is also the one in which they find themselves as adults. This question is distinct from whether the economic standing of individuals is the same from one generation to the next.

Possible solutions to the sparse data problem include better surveys, linking surveys to administrative records, and building exclusively and directly on administrative data, such as those from the Internal Revenue Service and the Social Security Administration. Grusky argued for the latter approach, because it would generate an extremely large data set that would facilitate cross-group comparisons, permit analyses of term income histories that better approximate permanent income, make detailed occupations available and linkable to those of dependent children, and provide data on family structure and (imputed) wealth. Of course administrative records data have limitations, but Grusky believes the quality of the data would improve over the long run if monitoring efforts were dependent on them.

He then discussed the merits of having a standardized measure of intergenerational mobility. Detractors argue that it would saddle the field with a problematic standard and suppress innovation. The alternative view is that some sort of national measurement system for monitoring mobility would in fact inspire more critical research. Whether more research is beneficial depends on the opportunity cost, that is, what other research is being squeezed out that is more important to pursue.

DISCUSSION

In discussing these presentations, Christine Bachrach observed that a number of concepts (e.g., marital status, social mobility, poverty) have been characterized as Ballungen. In some cases there are concepts that truly are not precisely defined, like happiness. But some of the others seem amenable to disaggregation into very precisely defined smaller components. In the case of marital status, it appeared to her that new meanings were being tagged to a measure and a concept that is actually very precisely defined. Marriage is a legal status, precisely defined by law. She questioned whether introducing such dimensions as living arrangements, relationship stability, and relationship status into marital status might lead to the creation of a definition that is unnecessarily imprecise.

Nancy Cartwright responded that, for many concepts, it is certainly possible to provide more precise definitions, which is necessary for making scientifically defensible comparisons and tracking changes. Bradburn added that the more one defines a concept precisely for scientific purposes, the further it can depart from its originally intended meaning and the rich everyday concept that people think it means. On one hand, with respect to poverty, Cartwright suggested, it might be more helpful to simply have the array of poverty definitions available if the ordinary concept of poverty is not described properly by any single one of them. On the other hand, on specific occasions one of the definitions might be the right one to use.

David Johnson (U.S. Census Bureau) raised a question about the lack of a single accepted disability measure. He observed that there is a disability rate to evaluate health outcomes, a disability rate to evaluate employment outcomes, and a disability rate to evaluate adherence to the Americans with Disabilities Act. Bradburn responded that there would be different measures depending on the purpose, that there may not be one perfect measure. Michael endorsed the idea of increasing transparency and clarity by posting a whole range of estimates and letting analysts pick the right one for their purposes.

MEASURING AND MODELING OF SELF-REGULATION: IS STANDARDIZATION A REASONABLE GOAL?

Compared with the concepts of poverty and intergenerational mobility, Rick Hoyle (Duke University) observed, the concept of self-regulation has no apparent consequences for politics, at least at this point in time. The implications of standardization and the adoption of a common metric would in this case have far more to do with the accumulation of evidence in the progress of science than it does for policy. As a social psychologist, Hoyle had not really considered the likely payoff or the impediments to thinking about a shared understanding even of how things might be measured. In fact, the field of social psychology is more likely to place value on originality and creativity in developing alternative ways to measure concepts. There is not even a hint of movement that he has discerned to standardize the measure of self-regulation. Instead, he approached his presentation as a thought exercise to ask whether there is value to moving toward a common understanding of the construct and how it should be measured.

Hoyle described self-regulation as a relatively new construct that has become of increasing interest from both a scientific and a lay perspective, and it will become increasingly important, for example as an education policy topic. He dated empirical research on the topic back to the late 1960s, with the first bona fide theoretical model appearing in 1972. Self-regulation is primarily a topic of study in social psychology, with applications in clinical psychology/psychiatry, education, and increasingly other areas that relate to goal-directed behavior—for example, a general theory of crime, lack of self-control, health behavior, sport, and delinquency. There has been a rapid increase in use of the construct, currently accumulating at a rate of about 120 published articles per year. As evidence has accumulated, social psychologists have begun to pull together handbooks that summarize the state of the art, with a total of 114 chapters published in the last 10 years on the topic of self-regulation.

He attributed the increased interest in part to a number of developments that exemplify lack of self-regulation: (1) the significant amount of U.S. consumers' revolving credit debt, (2) rising obesity rates, and (3) the recent economic crisis, which is attributable in part to excessive borrowing and lending and high-risk investments made with little or no concern for potential long-term consequences.

It is difficult for Hoyle to imagine how he might have a measure without a model. However, it is very clear to him that there is no commonly accepted model of self-regulation at this time. Although there is currently no consensus regarding even its definition, a working definition of self-regulation might be the various means by which human beings manage themselves, including the following:

- Attention—the degree to which one is able to stay focused on an important task in the face of distraction;
- Cognition—the degree to which one is able to produce positive thoughts or suppress negative thoughts when distressed;
- Motivation—finding the will to continue in the face of challenge and stopping when continuing is unlikely to produce a desired outcome;
- Emotion—seeking or prolonging pleasant emotions and resisting or quickly banishing unpleasant emotions; and
- Behavior—for example, declining a second helping of food when it is offered, going to the gym when it is inconvenient or requires sacrificing preferred behavior.

In each of these systems, Hoyle noted two conceptual distinctions; first, the idea of self-stopping and self-starting and, second, the idea of deliberate versus automatic actions.

Hoyle next provided evidence of the predictive potency of self-regulation from three research studies. Building on earlier studies on children's ability to self-regulate by delaying gratification, Walter Mischel and colleagues (1989) found that preschool delay time predicted a number of fairly consequential outcomes, including academic and social competence, coping ability, and personality characteristics in adolescence (e.g., greater attentiveness, planfulness, and reasoning ability). Caspi and Moffitt's large-scale birth cohort study revealed that children who were considered "under-controlled" at age 3 were, at age 18, high on impulsivity, danger-seeking, and various other traits that are related to poor self-control; at age 21, some 18 years after their initial assessment, they were more than twice as likely than their counterparts to engage in a variety of problem behaviors. Finally, James Heckman's research on early deficits in self-regulation found that they translate to reduced personal, social, and economic productivity in adulthood. Heckman posits that early childhood investments that narrow the gap in noncognitive abilities can offer a ninefold return on investment, yielding a 15-17 percent increase in adult economic productivity and making a compelling case for early intervention.

In the continuum between metric diversity and common metrics, the concept of self-regulation is clearly in the direction of metric diversity. In the literature, one finds most data generated by small-scale experiments and three types of measures of self-regulation in use: rating scale measures,[2] personality inventories, and measures derived from behavior.

The advantages of rating scale measures include their focus specifically on self-regulation and the frequent use of multiple subscales that allow for fine-grained assessment of the construct. Personality inventories, generally for adolescents and adults, were not originally designed to measure self-regulation, but they often include subscales addressing it (conscientiousness and constraint being two personality dimensions that are clearly relevant) that are so widely used that normative data are typically available. Apart from these normative comparisons, neither the rating scale measures nor the personality inventories have inherent meaning. Both require self-reports and are generally suitable only for adolescents and adults. Hoyle took issue with the reliance on self-reports, given the evidence that people are poor at reporting their own mental states, and the inability to track self-regulation over the life course beginning at much earlier ages.

Measures derived from behavior are typically generated in small-scale controlled experiments. Examples include duration of self-imposed delay, control of emotional expression when exposed to emotion-invoking stimuli, pain tolerance, and inhibition of interference. These measures offer a number of advantages, including their reliance on observable behavior (i.e., self-reports are not required) and the facts that situations can be devised that generate scores even for young children, and that the metrics often have inherent meaning (e.g., time, number of attempts). However, there is no generally accepted paradigm, behaviors are likely to reflect other constructs in addition to self-regulation, and there are no manipulation checks. As a result, Hoyle stated, it is difficult to know whether a finding should be attributed to self-regulation or to some other construct that one has unwittingly manipulated.

Hoyle's review of current measurement approaches indicates that there is no existing measure that stands out as particularly promising for developing a standardized metric. Rather than "habitual measurement" and "seductions of theory," Hoyle saw the concept of self-regulation characterized by ad hoc measures and "seductions of novelty." Social psychologists gain notoriety when they coin a new term or develop a measure that is somehow

---

[2]Examples of rating scale measures include the Self-Regulation Questionnaire ("I am able to accomplish goals I set for myself"), the Self-Control & Self-Management Scale ("I keep focused on tasks I need to do even if I do not like them"), the Self-Control Schedule, the Good & Poor Self-Control Scales, the Ego-Control/Ego-Resiliency Scales, the Self-Control Scale, and the Self-Control Rating Scale.

different from what is currently in the books. This culture works against standardization and common metrics. It also is not clear what the form of a standard measure should be (e.g., global, domain-specific), nor what quality of self-regulation matters most (e.g., capacity, style, capability). The focus has been on process rather than classification.

He summarized what he considered features of a desirable metric. It must be intuitive, that is, phrased in terms that have inherent meaning. The units should have basis in commonly accepted reality, so that change can be expressed in meaningful units. And finally, the metric must have the same meaning across the range of characteristics on which comparisons would be made (e.g., preschool to adulthood). He saw a number of advantages to standardization: (1) the results across studies and research programs could be compared, (2) empirical evidence would more readily and quickly accumulate, (3) the construct might be more likely to be assessed or discussed routinely outside the academy, thus drawing social psychologists more into discussions of social issues and into informing policy development and evaluation.

Hoyle recognized that there are many reasons why standardization may not be a good idea at a particular time. When no measure is a candidate for widespread use, the use of multiple measures can help to triangulate a construct and test the robustness of effects across operational definitions. He also appreciated the benefits of mid-range models, that is, models that spring up for different reasons and are not really trying to serve as a comprehensive explanation for self-regulation. He feared that standardization might thwart this, because it would be unlikely that a single measure would map onto and satisfy the needs of every given approach to thinking about the construct. A standardized approach might also shift examination away from process, which he thought would be a mistake at this point in the history of the construct. As evidence accumulates, models can be integrated, trimmed, and simplified.

Hoyle drew a number of lessons from his review of self-regulation measures:

- Standardization does not seem necessary for a research literature to thrive or for research funding.
- Without convergence on a common model or set of prominent features of the construct, there can be no convergence on a common metric.
- Pressure to standardize measurement at this time would stymie research on process, continued refinement of the construct, and operational definitions.
- Without standardization or a common metric, the construct rarely enters into discussions of social issues and social policy.

- Although attempts at standardization would be premature, there are advantages to working toward standardization and a common metric while allowing metric diversity to continue.

DISCUSSION

Rebecca Maynard (University of Pennsylvania) said that the presentations in this session collectively have done a good job of modeling what is often desirable, and sometimes not, about common metrics in the social sciences. They also illustrated for her the limitations of moving too quickly to common metrics. She then made a number of observations.

She first observed that even when the science and technology for developing common metrics exist, there is a time and place for common metrics. Cartwright and Bradburn (2010) laid out a three-step process of defining what is to be measured, selecting the metric for measuring it, and applying the metric. These same steps are also the gatekeepers demarking readiness for common metrics. The current poverty index came about because there was a readiness—a need in the war on poverty, a ready metric, and an ability to apply that metric. There has been little progress to change this measure—despite very good work by NRC and other researchers demonstrating all the pitfalls of the current measures and other ways to measure poverty better—not only in large part because of inertia, but also because there has been no compelling reason to adopt an alternative.

One of the areas in which Maynard hopes common metrics will be developed is what she termed 21st-century skills, which are skills needed to improve the labor market readiness of those at the bottom of the skills distribution and national productivity. Such vocational skills include aspects of self-regulation (or social competence), the ability to take direction, and reading. It seemed to her that the research literature may provide a strong foundation for understanding what to measure as well as the psychometric capacity to develop such a metric. Although none of the papers explicitly cautioned against creating common measures "before their time," she believes that the papers by Grusky and Hoyle came close.

Maynard next observed that there is a temptation to clump concepts—the things to be measured—under neat labels and to want common measures for them. In some cases, she surmised, consensus and utility might be much quicker to achieve for narrower concepts. In each of the three domains considered in this session—poverty, social mobility, and self-regulation—the concepts to be measured could well be context specific. She noted Michael's point about why different definitions of poverty might be needed or different measures advantageous if the intent is to apply the measure cross-nationally. The concept of poverty also might differ if the focus is on children, prime age adults, or the elderly. Similarly, she noted Grusky's compelling examples of the theoretical and practical implications of different definitions of social mobility. For example, what to measure and the appropriate metrics would be different for understanding and comparing social status and relationships intergenerationally than if the purpose is to monitor and promote equal opportunity in education or economic welfare.

In Maynard's view, Hoyle made a convincing case that for self-regulation there is neither a compelling need for a common metric nor is it likely that there would ever be a need for a single measure. The concept of self-regulation varies with age, with setting, and with goal. It is an umbrella concept that, for scientific, political, and practical purposes, would probably need to be greatly refined and tailored to the intended use.

For Maynard, one of the implications from this meeting is that it would be desirable to embark on a strategy of encouraging and facilitating the use of common metrics in cases in which there are well-established, meaningful metrics or when such measures could be constructed and made accessible with reasonable effort. This could take the form of doing a better job of ensuring that the good metrics are well defined, have established psychometric properties, and that the means for application of these measures is in the public domain. Royalties for the use of measures would be a deterrent to adoption, regardless of their quality.

Maynard also shared three smaller observations

1. The process of developing common metrics will be facilitated by encouraging the adoption of common items (anchor items) that can provide cross-walks across studies that are using different measures of similar constructs intentionally—for example, because their contexts or purposes differ or because they are still working on good measure development.
2. Greater use of "linking" studies could and should be encouraged when there is an interest in comparing across studies or data sets using different measures of purportedly the same construct, like poverty or social mobility.
3. It may be necessary to change the incentive structure for the scientific community to discourage the creation of new measures for the wrong reasons, such as to advance a professional career or for financial gain. More thought needs to be given to rewarding researchers for replicating and extending and to the relevance of the measures and the metrics.

OPEN DISCUSSION

Sheila Jasanoff (Harvard University) began the discussion by asking whether there is benefit to thinking about standardization itself as being on some sort of conceptual sliding scale. There seems to be a gradation in the level of social articulation at which a concept, construct, or ontology develops. She questioned if different conceptual unpacking could be employed to avoid using one word across very different kinds of domains of the social sciences and their relationship to policy. One might also think of standardization as potentially a form of social production or reproduction that relates to the evolution of the construct itself.

Grusky said that it is important to know how a particular construct is being used in public discourse (e.g., social mobility) and the way in which the science itself has proceeded. For social mobility, the field has recognized that the concept is best understood in a more disaggregated form. He believes it is possible to demand precision in the scientific context by recognizing that there are quite distinct and important types of mobility, all of which should be monitored simultaneously and operationalized in a credible way and also combined into a single model in order to tease out the relationships among different types.

Robert Pollak commented on the idea of deconstructing concepts into more distinguishable pieces. For example, he found it interesting to consider two distinct concepts inherent in self-regulation—self-regulation of attention and self-regulation of behavior—that might be measured separately. He cautioned against standardization if it means imposing a unitary or dual construction from the outside in a bureaucratic way. In Grusky's view, standardization may be seen as a kind of correct representation of the simultaneous consideration of constructs and measures that are now independent.

Turning to the notion of intergenerational mobility, Pollak observed that much of the early literature on intergenerational mobility assumed that people were raised in two-parent families, and the main focus was on transmission from fathers to sons. This formulation is no longer appropriate in the context of changing family structures, for example the growing prevalence of female-headed families, nonmarital fertility, and the effects of immigration. Grusky agreed with Pollak on the importance of factoring in mother's income and occupation; ignoring mother's occupation will result in profound misunderstanding about the direction of the trend in intergenerational mobility in the family.

Pollak also remarked that although there is no standardization between economics and sociology, the collection of data essentially involves choices about which questions to ask. In collecting income and occupational data, there is no requirement that the users of the data must focus on the occupations piece or the earnings piece. Agreeing on the type of data to collect could be another way of promoting common metrics.

Robert Hauser returned to the issue of self-regulation. He stated that the economists' original notion of ability in human capital was a very global concept: whatever was left over in the psychology of individuals. The arrival of easily accessible data from IQ tests created a huge market for the use of IQ as the "ability" in economic models of education and educational and economic success. This resulted in a dominant line of interest involving the consequences of cognitive ability. There is now a research program centered in Scotland looking at the correlation between IQ and mortality (which appears all over the world), but there is nothing in the literature that explains why the correlation occurs. Hauser argued that it is exceptionally important to have a few widely accepted measures of self-regulation. In the Wisconsin Longitudinal Study, Hauser has looked at the IQ-mortality relationship over a span of 52 years from ages 18 to 68 and found the expected relationship, which he attributes to a simple explanation: the effect of IQ is completely mediated by rank in high school class, which he believes is closely tied to self-regulation, conscientiousness, dependability, and other regularities in behavior. He further argued that there is a compelling public interest to get the story straight. To accomplish this, widely accepted metrics are required. He noted that this was also true years ago of social standing and occupational standing. Rather than novelty, he believes that something socially useful, which helps to nail down narrowly defined cognitive measures, will make a difference in people's lives. Hoyle agreed with Hauser but was not clear how to move to a widely accepted measure of self-regulation.

Rick Moser (National Cancer Institute) was intrigued by the idea of creating incentives for the use of standardized measures. A psychologist by training, he understands the rewards for innovation in his field but expressed concern that psychology specifically has suffered as a result in the building of cumulative knowledge. The National Cancer Institute is creating a tool to facilitate standardization and has questioned how to create incentives for the use of standardized measures, especially in light of the competing rewards acting against this. He recognizes that some constructs and associated measures are not ready for standardization, but he questioned at what point refinement needs to stop and use begin.

Maynard sought to discover ways to encourage people to start with the best, most relevant measure, improve on it using new data, and ultimately create cross-walks between studies. She also encouraged making data sets publicly available after publication. Funding agencies can help by requiring that contractors and grantees draw on what exists or justify why they need to deviate. Widespread adoption of measures is more likely if the measures are publicly or readily available. Maynard said she is aware of a major ongoing initiative of the Department of Education for a compendium of measures; other federal agencies also support similar efforts.

George Bohrnstedt also thinks that federal agencies can be influential in pushing for cooperative agreements and use of common measures. Hoyle observed that the problem can be one of framing, not just incentives. Once the frame shifts from the impact of "my" work to the impact of "our" work, then there must be some agreement on what it is we are doing, why we are doing it, and how we do it. Moser observed that this type of effort is challenging because it requires an altruistic stance on behalf of the field.

In thinking of the criteria for standardization on one hand, and the coherence and robustness of the metric on the other, Geoff Mulgan pointed to the need for some assessment of how the standardized metric will be used and also the cost of not having a standardized metric. He supplied three examples that follow from the comments above.

1. Social mobility is at the moment very politically contested, in the United Kingdom and in other countries, because of cross-national studies appearing to show deceleration or stagnation of social mobility. However, there is no agreement about the appropriate statistics and their meaning, and this is impeding basic democratic debate about what society should do about the issue. Even an imperfect indicator can be important to allow a society to have a competent discussion about proper actions to take.

2. There is a traditional materialist bias in all the poverty measures that no longer resonates with what poverty really means or with essentially abundant societies in which social support and psychological needs matter as much as material needs. This disjuncture makes it difficult for society to have a serious conversation about what should be done about need and undermines the legitimacy of actions that appear to follow from the measures. Again, Mulgan would rather have a good-enough set of reasonably widely agreed-on measures than perfect agreement on a measure that does not fit with the underlying public discourse on the issues.

3. He is involved in setting up a network of schools that emphasizes the development of social intelligence, self-regulation, and cognitive skills. The effort must demonstrate success to a very metric-focused school system. There is an urgent need for a good-enough metric, which may be one or two measures of self-regulation. The school system cannot wait 5-10 years for the perfect metric. He called for consideration of the conditions acceptable for creating measures that are imperfect but good enough.

Grusky contended that the case for standardization could be made more forcefully, particularly in social mobility. He noted that the Pew Charitable Trusts is supporting an economic mobility project and is actively publicizing the results. If it were to make its measures official, they could be better than good enough as standardized measures. Grusky believes such an effort could crystallize the best that can be found in the scientific community, and having a national mobility accounting framework would be the impetus to go beyond good enough to a gold standard.

Turning to poverty measures, Michael vehemently disagreed with the notion that there is no compelling reason to adopt a better poverty measure. He believes the standard currently in use in the United States is embarrassing and illogical, and there clearly are many intellectually superior alternatives. In his view, the obstacle is not inertia but politics. He expressed frustration that *Measuring Poverty*, the work of NRC from 15 years ago, has not realized much traction.

In survey data activities, Michael supported the idea of linking to administrative records, since this could reduce costs by reducing survey time and increase the size of the samples.

Revisiting the distinction between standardization and harmonization, Michael viewed standardization as top-down and harmonization as bottom-up. In his view, people will adopt measures that work well for their purposes, and he favored reliance on competition in the marketplace of ideas. He emphasized that science is all about standardizations established among scientists, not imposed on them. He therefore did not see that the benefits of imposed standardization outweigh the costs—quite the contrary.

5

Final Comments

In the final session, Miron Straf (National Research Council) made a list of some of the themes articulated by participants during the workshop:

- Good measurement begins with the end in mind. If common metrics are the goal, it is important to consider both their purpose and criteria.
- One size does not fit all. In this regard, the goal may not be common metrics per se, but rather a few metrics widely used.
- Common metrics require common concepts—which are facilitated by agreement on theory.
- The issue may not be so much what is measured as how it is perceived and classified. Ontology is very important.
- Useful standardization is balanced with construct validity.
- Just as perception can trump reality, politics trumps science. And public and political demands can trump scientific review.
- Some measures defy standardization—such as self-regulation and social class.
- Measures will need to change over time because concepts do, and in particular what is considered important changes over time.
- Raw data—whether collected, compiled, or pooled—may be grist for the measurement mill, but they do not become refined in that mill. Data in their disaggregated form are often more useful than a metric.
- Meta-analysis is no substitute for primary analysis.
- Useful social science needs measures that are widely accepted.

George Bohrnstedt repeated some of his challenges to the group to consider when standardization makes sense. Is there a set of criteria? When does it not make sense to standardize? What are the costs from not standardizing? Even when there is benefit to standardization, the incentives to develop common metrics may be inadequate, especially in some fields in which academic reputations are built on development of a new method, concept, or construct.

Norman Bradburn observed that the question of the importance of standardization has two parts: (1) When does it make a difference and when is it useful for science? (2) When is it useful for policy issues? On the science side, when concepts are sufficiently well defined and theory is sufficiently well formulated, then standardization is important. In terms of metric or procedures, confidence that the same construct is being measured is important for advancing theory. He further observed that the lack of overall theory about psychological processes has led to a reward structure that places a premium on inventing new measures.

On the policy side, Bradburn elaborated on the use of measures of the effectiveness of social, economic, or educational policies and the push in the last decades toward accountability. He commented that any measure (like the current poverty measure) that is insensitive to the policy lever used to change it seems to be a bad measure. It would seem that any politician should want to effectively measure improvements to demonstrate program success.

Bohrnstedt agreed that science and politics have roles to play. Politics trumps science. What can the academic community do to mobilize action? In response to this question, David Grusky commented that society must choose where it wants politics to intrude in policy decisions. There can be a cacophony of measures, and politics will intrude in deciding which measure to feature. Or alternatively, science could advocate for some official standard measure, and then politics will intrude on the selection of that measure. At least the latter is a more transparent process, which gives scientists an opportunity to provide input.

Bohrnstedt revisited the two measures of intergenerational mobility— one social, one economic—that society cares immensely about in its efforts to reduce inequality. He believes that having good measures of social mobility and economic mobility that draw on administrative records is a good idea. Education is ultimately about a way to reduce inequality and to facilitate intergenerational mobility. Grusky believes that when there is more transparency, there is more opportunity for the scientific community to weigh in at the point of adoption of some sort of official standardized measurement.

Dennis Fryback questioned what is meant by standardization, specifically in the health care context, and focused on the difference between classical and modern test theory. The notion that standardization means adoption of the same questions is passé. It may be that the latent constructs that hearken back to theory are what need to be standardized. He is most familiar with more parochial politics about the appropriate survey questions. In contrast, the Patient-Reported Outcomes Measurement Information System lets everyone see their questions in the item bank, and it transcends the single questionnaire. He questioned whether there could be a common construct underlying different definitions of poverty if different measures of poverty could be subjected to item response theory–type analysis.

Bohrnstedt reaffirmed the idea that having common concepts does not mean that the indicators will not change over time. He cited the view, expressed by Geoff Mulgan, that indicators should change over time because they are culture- and history-bound, although the concepts should remain the same.

David Johnson suggested that researchers align themselves with policy makers and statistical agencies to develop standardized measures, accepting that a perfect measure (e.g., for poverty) is sometimes not possible. He pointed to work currently being undertaken by the Census Bureau to measure same-sex marriage (in which decisions are being made today for implementation in eight years) and vocational education. The Census Bureau has solicited advice about developing a measure that may not be perfect. As an indication of progress, he reported that there is a provision of $7.5 million in the president's budget that directs the Census Bureau to develop a new supplemental poverty measure. Robert Pollak was not nearly so optimistic about the adoption of new poverty measures; changing the definition will change eligibility for benefits, he said. There are strong constituencies that will resist this type of change.

Bradburn mentioned three ways in which major indicators become accepted. First, he noted that the poverty measure is implemented by the Office of Management and Budget (OMB), whereas the employment rate is implemented by the Bureau of Labor Statistics.[1] If responsibility for a measure is lodged in the domain of the president's office (e.g., OMB), it is likely to be politicized. If responsibility is lodged in one of the statistical agencies, where the decision makers are generally science professionals, it will be easier to change the measure (if it is done by the government). Second, some very farsighted scientists can set about constructing a measure before it is needed—an example is the National Assessment of Educational Progress (NAEP)—and the measure can become adopted as the accepted measure before it becomes politicized. For NAEP this was largely done by

---

[1]Bradburn attributed this insight to a talk by Rebecca Blank at the American Statistical Association in August 2009.

the private sector. Finally, a bipartisan public-private effort referred to as SUSA (State of the USA) publicizes on a regular basis a set of indicators across all sectors of economics and society and the environment, in an effort to inform the democratic process. So there is attention to making some indicators easily available to the broad public.

Geoff Mulgan said that it is helpful to consider the three sets of interest groups: the scientific community, the government, and the public. In his view, the scientific community has an obligation to itself, to science, and to a degree to the public but not to the state. The closer any indicator gets to being used for actual administrative decisions, as with the poverty indicator, the less appropriate it is for the scientific community to lend its legitimacy to it because of the risks of distortion. However, to treat any indicator as essentially a feedback system, there are different interests in place as to what counts as good feedback. For the scientific community, there is a lengthy time scale, cumulative knowledge, etc. For the public, one of the criteria could be whether to hold the state to account. Mulgan observed that different indicators will respond to these three interests in different ways at different times.

Arthur Kendall (U.S. General Accounting Office, retired) shared his perspective as a social psychologist and mathematical statistician. He advised that when dealing with a concept in a particular construct, it is important to look across disciplines to see what connotations and denotations the terms have in other disciplines. Ontology could be semantics. It is important to pay attention to how other people are using the concepts. He believes that an important role of the scientific community is to facilitate communications among the disciplines and between the disciplines and the policy, intelligence, government, and current administration and congressional groups. He added that if something is incomplete, that does not mean it is wrong. He also pointed to the importance of level of analysis—for example, a change in the number of children counted as proficient is not the same as a change in the number of those whose proficiency has changed.

Robert Hauser underscored the importance of persistence in getting a measure accepted. Measurement breakthroughs can take a long time. The fundamental measurement work that showed how old the universe is and that it is expanding was based on measurements that began in 1974. Another example is *Measuring Poverty*, the 1995 National Research Council report. It has persisted and perhaps may yet have the kind of effect that was originally intended. There was recently action in Congress to move it forward, championed by Mayor Michael Bloomberg in New York. A third example is the addition of occupational mobility questions to the Survey of Income and Program Participation (SIPP). Despite initial sentiments that there was no national interest in measuring social mobility, Hauser and his colleagues succeeded in adding three questions to the SIPP on this topic. He believes it is time to try again to add more questions.

To move ahead, Matthew Snipp recognizes the need to decide what can be and what should be standardized. Even if standardization is not possible, harmonization might be, especially across time and space. He called for the participation of another set of actors—representatives of statistical agencies, the Association of Public Data Users, the Council of Professional Associations on Federal Statistics, among others—who have a direct interest in the production of federal statistics and are proactive in making their views known. Bohrnstedt agreed that harmonization could be possible when standardization is not. He noted, for example, that in the National Center for Education Statistics, various measures of social class or social economic status are used. He welcomed greater efforts by U.S. statistical agencies to harmonize measures across agencies at a given point in time, so that different statistical agencies, or different units in the same statistical agency, are not measuring the same construct or concept in vastly different ways.

References

Bohrnstedt, G.W. (2010). *An overview of measurement in the social sciences.* Paper prepared for the Workshop on Advancing Social Science Theory: The Importance of Common Metrics. National Academies, Washington, DC, February 25-26.

Cartwright, N.L., and Bradburn, N.M. (2010). *Measurement for science and policy.* Paper prepared for the Workshop on Advancing Social Science Theory: The Importance of Common Metrics. National Academies, Washington, DC, February 25-26.

Caspi, A., and Silva, P.A. (1995). Temperamental qualities at age 3 predict personality traits in young adulthood: Longitudinal evidence from a birth cohort. *Child Development, 66,* 486-498.

Caspi, A., Gegg, D., Dickson, N., Harrington, H., Langley, J., Moffitt, T.E., and Silva, P.A. (1997). Personality differences predict health-risk behaviors in young adulthood: Evidence from a longitudinal study. *Journal of Personality and Social Psychology, 73,* 1052-1063.

Deaton, A., and Heston, A. (2010). Understanding PPPs and PPP-based national accounts. *American Economic Journal: Macroeconomics, 2*(4), 1-35.

Diewert, W.E., Greenlees, J.S., and Hulten, C.R. (2009). *Price index concepts and measurement.* Chicago: University of Chicago Press.

Duncan, O.D. (1961). A socioeconomic index for all occupations. In A.J. Reiss, Jr. (Ed.), *Occupations and Social Status* (pp. 109-38). New York: Free Press.

Duncan, O.D. (1984). *Notes on social measurement: Historical and critical.* New York: Russell Sage Foundation.

Erikson, R., and Goldthorpe, J.H. (1992). *The constant flux: A study of class mobility in industrial societies.* Oxford, Eng.: Clarendon Press.

Fabricant, S. (1984). Toward a firmer basis of economic policy: The founding of the National Bureau of Economic Research. Cambridge, MA: National Bureau of Economic Research. Available: http://www.nber.org/nberhistory/sfabricantrev.pdf [accessed July 2, 2010].

Fryback, D.G. (2010). *Measuring health-related quality of life.* Paper prepared for the Workshop on Advancing Social Science Theory: The Importance of Common Metrics. National Academies, Washington, DC, February 25-26.

Fryback, D.G., Palta, M., Cherepanov, D., Bolt, D., and Kim, J.S. (2010). Comparison of 5 health-related quality of life indexes using item response theory analysis. *Medical Decision Making, 30*(1), 5-15.

Ganzeboom, H.B., De Graaf, P.M., and Treiman, D.J. (1992). A standard international socioeconomic index of occupational status. *Social Science Research, 21*, 1-56.

Grusky, D.B., and Cumberworth, E. (2010). *A national protocol for measuring intergenerational mobility?* Paper prepared for the Workshop on Advancing Social Science Theory: The Importance of Common Metrics. National Academies, Washington, DC, February 25-26.

Guttman, L. (1950). The basis for scalogram analysis. In S. Stouffer et al. (Eds.), *Measurement and prediction*. The American Soldier Vol. IV. New York: Wiley.

Hauser, R.M. (2010). *Comparable metrics: Some examples.* Paper prepared for the Workshop on Advancing Social Science Theory: The Importance of Common Metrics. National Academies, Washington, DC, February 25-26.

Hauser, R.M., Warren, J.R., Huang, M.-H., and Carter, W.Y. (2000). Occupational status, education, and social mobility in the meritocracy. In K. Arrow, S. Bowles, and S. Durlauf (Eds.), *Meritocracy and economic inequality* (pp. 179-229). Princeton, NJ: Princeton University Press.

Heckman, J.J. (2006). Skill formation and the economics of investing in disadvantaged children. *Science, 312*, 1900-1902.

Hollingshead, A.G. (1957). *Two-factor index of social position.* New Haven: Yale University Press.

Hoyle, R.H., and Bradfield, E.K. (2010). *Measurement and modeling of self-regulation: Is standardization a reasonable goal?* Paper prepared for the Workshop on Advancing Social Science Theory: The Importance of Common Metrics. National Academies, Washington, DC, February 25-26.

King, G., Murray, C.J.L., Salomon, J.A., and Tandon, A. (2004). Enhancing the validity of cross-cultural comparability of survey research. *American Political Science Review, 98*, 191-207.

Koopmans, T.C. (1947). Measurement without theory. *Review of Economics and Statistics, 29*(3), 161-172. Available at http://cowles.econ.yale.edu/P/cp/p00a/p0025a.pdf [accessed July 2, 2010].

McHorney, C.A. (1999). Health status assessment methods for adults: Past accomplishments and future challenges. *Annual Review of Public Health, 20*, 309-335.

Michael, R.T. (2010). *Measuring poverty: the question of standardization.* Paper prepared for the Workshop on Advancing Social Science Theory: The Importance of Common Metrics. National Academies, Washington, DC, February 25-26.

Miech, R.A., and Hauser, R.M. (2001). Socioeconomic status (SES) and health at midlife: A comparison of educational attainment with occupation-based indicators. *Annals of Epidemiology, 11*, 75-84.

Mischel, W., Shoda, Y., and Rodriguez, M.L. (1989). Delay of gratification in children. *Science, 244*, 933-938.

Molla, M., Wagener, D.K., and Madans, J.H. (2001). Summary measures of population health: Methods for calculating health expectancy. *Healthy People Statistical Notes No. 21.* Hyattsville, MD: National Center for Health Statistics.

Mulgan, G. (2010). *Advantages and disadvantages of the standardization of indicators used in policy.* Paper prepared for the Workshop on Advancing Social Science Theory: The Importance of Common Metrics. National Academies, Washington, DC, February 25-26.

National Governors Association. (2008). *Implementing graduation counts: State progress to date, 2008.* Washington, DC: National Governors Association Center for Best Practices.

National Research Council. (1982). *Behavioral and social science research: A national resource, Part 1.* Committee on Basic Research in the Behavioral and Social Sciences, R.M. Adams, N.J. Smelser, and D.J. Treiman, (Eds.). Washington, DC: National Academy Press.

National Research Council. (1995). *Measuring poverty: A new approach.* Panel on Poverty and Family Assistance: Concepts, Information Needs, and Measurement Methods, C.F. Citro and R.T. Michael (Eds.). Washington, DC: National Academy Press.

National Research Council. (1996). *Spotlight on heterogeneity: The federal standards for racial and ethnic classification.* Committee on National Statistics. Washington, DC: National Academy Press.

National Research Council. (2005). *Measuring literacy: Performance levels for adults.* Committee on Performance Levels for Adult Literacy, R.M. Hauser, C.F. Edley, Jr., J.A. Koenig, and S.W. Elliott (Eds.). Washington, DC: The National Academies Press.

Patrick, D.L., and Erickson, P. (1993). *Health status and health policy: Quality of life in health care evaluation and resource allocation.* Oxford, Eng.: Oxford University Press.

Pollak, R.A. (2010). *Standardized measurement.* Paper prepared for the Workshop on Advancing Social Science Theory: The Importance of Common Metrics. National Academies, Washington, DC, February 25-26.

Prewitt, K. (1987). Public statistics and democratic politics. In W. Alonso and P. Starr (Eds.), *The politics of numbers* (pp. 113-128). New York: Russell Sage Foundation.

Shinn Jr., M. (1969). An application of pyschophysical scaling techniques to the measurement of national power. *Journal of Politics, 31,* 932-951.

Snipp, C.M. (2010). *Measuring race (and ethnicity).* Paper prepared for the Workshop on Advancing Social Science Theory: The Importance of Common Metrics. National Academies, Washington, DC, February 25-26.

Treiman, D.J. (1976). A standard occupational prestige scale for use with historical data. *Journal of Interdisciplinary History, 7,* 283-304.

Warren, R. (2010). *High school completion rates.* Paper prepared for the Workshop on Advancing Social Science Theory: The Importance of Common Metrics. National Academies, Washington, DC, February 25-26.

Willis, R.J. (2010). *Standardization of measurement: What can we learn from the economic sciences?* Paper prepared for the Workshop on Advancing Social Science Theory: The Importance of Common Metrics. National Academies, Washington, DC, February 25-26.

Wright, E.O. 1993. Typologies, scales, and class analysis: A comment on Halaby and Weakliem. *American Sociological Review, 58,* 31-34.

Appendix A

Workshop Agenda and Participants

Workshop on Advancing Social Science Theory:
The Importance of Common Metrics

February 25-26, 2010
National Academies Keck Building
500 Fifth Street, N.W., Washington, DC

Thursday, February 25, 2010

8:30 a.m.   Working breakfast

Participants arriving early are encouraged to discuss work-shop issues over breakfast served in the meeting room.

9:00   Introduction and goals for the workshop

Miron L. Straf, Workshop Director
George W. Bohrnstedt, Workshop Chair

Overview

Chair: Harris Cooper, Duke University

9:15   An overview of measurement in the social sciences

George W. Bohrnstedt, American Institutes for Research

9:45   Comparable metrics: Some examples

Robert M. Hauser, Division of Behavioral and Social Sciences and Education, National Research Council, Washington, DC, and University of Wisconsin, Madison

10:15   Discussion

               Christine A. Bachrach

10:40   **Break**

Examples

11:05   What can we learn from the economic sciences?

               Robert J. Willis, University of Michigan

11:35   Measuring health-related quality of life

               Dennis Fryback, University of Wisconsin, Madison

12:05 p.m.   Discussion

               Jack E. Triplett, Brookings Institution
               Kathleen A. Cagney, University of Chicago

12:30   **Lunch**

               Lunch is available in the Academies' atrium cafeteria on the
               third floor.

1:30   Open discussion

Indicators

               Chair: Barbara Schneider, Michigan State University

2:10   Advantages and disadvantages of the standardization of indi-
               cators used in policy

               Geoff Mulgan, The Young Foundation

Examples

2:40   Standardized measurement

               Robert A. Pollak, Washington University, St. Louis,
               Missouri

3:35   High school completion rates

         John Robert Warren, University of Minnesota

4:05   Measuring race (and ethnicity)

         C. Matthew Snipp, Stanford University

4:35   Discussion

         Kenneth Prewitt, Columbia University

5:00   Open discussion

5:40   **Reception** (first floor foyer)

6:45   **Dinner** (participants and invited guests)

Friday, February 26

8:30 a.m.   Working breakfast

         Participants arriving early are encouraged to discuss workshop issues over breakfast served in the meeting room.

Social-science constructs

         Chair: Sheila Jasanoff, Harvard University

9:00   The theory of measurement

         Nancy D. Cartwright, University of California, San Diego, and London School of Economics and Political Science and
Norman M. Bradburn, National Opinion Research Center, University of Chicago

Examples

9:30   Measuring poverty: The question of standardization

         Robert T. Michael, University of Chicago

10:00   A national protocol for measuring intergenerational mobility?

               David B. Grusky, Stanford University

10:30   **Break**

10:50   Measuring and modeling of self-regulation: Is standardization
               a reasonable goal?

               Rick Hoyle, Duke University

11:20 a.m.   Discussion

               Rebecca A. Maynard, University of Pennsylvania

11:45   Open discussion

12:15 p.m.   Common themes and lessons

               Planning committee for the workshop

12:45   Final comments from participants and guests

1:15   **Adjourn**

               Lunch is available in the atrium cafeteria on the third floor.

WORKSHOP PARTICIPANTS

Ana Aizcorbe
Chief Economist
Bureau of Economic Analysis

Christine A. Bachrach
Visiting Scholar, Social Science
    Research Institute
Duke University
Research Professor, School of
    Behavioral and Social Sciences
University of Maryland

George W. Bohrnstedt
Senior Vice President for Research
    Emeritus
American Institutes for Research

John Bowers
Reporter
Caset Associates, Inc.

Norman M. Bradburn
Tiffany and Margaret Blake
    Distinguished Service Professor
    Emeritus
University of Chicago
Senior Fellow, National Opinion
    Research Center

Kathleen A. Cagney
Director, Population Research
    Center
Associate Professor, Department of
    Health Studies
The University of Chicago

Nancy D. Cartwright
Professor of Philosophy and
    Director, Center for Philosophy
    of Natural and Social Sciences
London School of Economics and
    Political Science
Professor of Philosophy
University of California, San Diego

Constance Citro
Director, Committee on National
    Statistics
The National Academies

Harris Cooper
Professor and Chair
Department of Psychology and
    Neuroscience
Duke University

Paul Courtney
Biomedical Informatics
    Coordinator
National Cancer Institute

Pamela Flattau
Science and Technology Policy
    Institute
Institute for Defense Analyses

Mary Frase
Deputy Assistant Director
Directorate for Social, Behavioral
    and Economic Sciences
National Science Foundation

Dennis Fryback
Professor Emeritus
School of Medicine and Public
    Health
University of Wisconsin, Madison

Robert Geelar

David B. Grusky
Professor, Department of Sociology
Stanford University

Charles Hatcher

Robert M. Hauser
Vilas Research Professor of
Sociology
Center for Demography of Health
and Aging
University of Wisconsin, Madison

Taissa Hauser
Senior Scientist Emeritus
University of Wisconsin, Madison

Lee Herring
Director of Public Affairs & Public
Information
American Sociological Association

Rick Hoyle
Professor, Department of
Psychology and Neuroscience
Duke University

Sheila Jasanoff
Pforzheimer Professor of Science
and Technology Studies
Kennedy School of Government
Harvard University

David S. Johnson
Chief, Housing and Household
Economic Statistics Division
U.S. Census Bureau

Karen Jones
Training, Research, and Evaluation
Specialist/Statistician
U.S. Customs and Border
Protection

Toshiko Kaneda
Senior Research Associate
Population Reference Bureau

Arthur J. Kendall
Retired, U.S. General Accounting
Office

James Kirby

Rose Maria Li
President and CEO
Rose Li and Associates, Inc.

Mark Mather
Associate Vice President, Domestic
Programs
Population Reference Bureau

Rebecca A. Maynard
University Trustee Professor of
Education and Social Policy
Graduate School of Education
University of Pennsylvania

Olga Mayorova
Postdoctoral Research Associate
Department of Geography and
Regional Development
University of Arizona

Robert T. Michael
Eliakim Hastings Moore
Distinguished Service Professor
Emeritus, Harris School of
Public Policy Studies
University of Chicago

Wilhelmine Miller
Associate Research Professor
Department of Health Policy
George Washington University

Richard Moser
Research Psychologist
Behavioral Research Program
Division of Cancer Control and
    Population Sciences
National Cancer Institute

Geoff Mulgan
Director
The Young Foundation
London, England

Natalia Pane
Managing Analyst
American Institutes of Research

Robert A. Pollak
Hernreich Distinguished Professor
    of Economics
John M. Olin School of Business
Washington University, St. Louis,
    Missouri

Kenneth Prewitt
Carnegie Professor of Public
    Affairs
Vice President for Global Centers
Columbia University

Barbara Schneider
John A. Hannah Distinguished
    Professor
College of Education and
    Department of Sociology
Michigan State University

C. Matthew Snipp
Burnet C. and Mildred Finley
    Wohlford Professor
Department of Sociology
Stanford University

Jack E. Triplett
Non-Resident Senior Fellow
Brookings Institution

John Robert Warren
Professor and Director of
    Undergraduate Studies
Department of Sociology
Minnesota Population Center
University of Minnesota

Robert J. Willis
Professor of Economics and
    Research Professor
Survey Research Center and the
    Population Studies Center
Institute for Social Research
University of Michigan

National Research Council Staff

Michael Feuer (until August 31,
    2010)
Executive Director
Division of Behavioral and Social
    Sciences and Education
    (DBASSE)

Miron L. Straf
Deputy Director
DBASSE

Kirsten Sampson Snyder
Senior Report Review Officer
DBASSE

Christina Maranto
Mirzayan Fellow
DBASSE

Dorothy Majewski
Administrative Assistant
DBASSE

Appendix B

Biographical Sketches of Committee Members, Workshop Speakers, and Workshop Discussants

George W. Bohrnstedt (*Chair*) is senior vice president for research emeritus at the American Institutes for Research, where he is involved in the development of new programs of research for the organization and brings a deep interest in education research and policy issues. He has had an interest in measurement in the social sciences throughout his professional career, growing out of his minor in educational psychology with an emphasis on tests and measurement. He currently chairs the National Center for Education Statistics' Validity Studies Panel for the National Assessment of Educational Progress. He has B.S., M.S., and Ph.D. degrees in sociology and a minor in educational psychology from the University of Wisconsin, Madison.

Christine A. Bachrach is a visiting scholar at the Social Science Research Institute at Duke University and research professor in the School of Behavioral and Social Sciences at the University of Maryland. Her scientific interests and publications span the areas of fertility, family formation, marriage and divorce, adoption, sexual behavior, contraceptive practice, population health, and survey methodology. Her current research focuses on the measurement and integration of cultural schemas in social demography. She has an M.A. in sociology from Georgetown University and a Ph.D. in population dynamics from Johns Hopkins University.

Norman M. Bradburn is Tiffany and Margaret Blake distinguished service professor emeritus of the University of Chicago and a senior fellow at the National Opinion Research Center (NORC). Associated with NORC

89

since 1961, he has been both director and president of its Board of Trustees. At the National Research Council, he has chaired the Committee on National Statistics, the panel to advise the Census Bureau on alternative methods for conducting the census in the year 2000, the panel to review the National Assessment of Educational Progress, and the panel to assess the 2000 census. Bradburn has a Ph.D. in social psychology from Harvard University.

Kathleen A. Cagney is associate professor in the Departments of Health Studies, Sociology, and Comparative Human Development at the University of Chicago. Her work examines social inequality and its relationship to health, with a focus on neighborhood, race, and aging and the life course. She is principal investigator of a study that explores neighborhood social context and its role in the health and well-being of older Chicagoans. She is director of the Population Research Center, codirector of the Center on the Demography and Economics of Aging, and a senior fellow at the National Opinion Research Center. She has a Ph.D. from Johns Hopkins University and an M.P.P. from the University of Chicago.

Nancy D. Cartwright is professor of philosophy in the Department of Philosophy, Logic and Scientific Method in the London School of Economics and Political Science; she is also professor of philosophy at the University of California, San Diego. Her principal interests are the philosophy and history of science (especially physics and economics), causal inference, and evidence and objectivity in science and policy. She is currently president of the Philosophy of Science Association and past president of the American Philosophical Association, Pacific Division. Cartwright has a Ph.D. in philosophy from the University of Illinois, Chicago.

Harris Cooper is professor of psychology and chair of the Department of Psychology and Neuroscience at Duke University. His work involves research syntheses and meta-analysis in varied fields, such as personality and social psychology, developmental psychology, marketing, and developmental medicine and child neurology, and the application of social and developmental psychology to education policy issues. He is past editor of the *Psychological Bulletin* and currently serves as the chief editorial adviser for the journals program of the American Psychological Association. He has a Ph.D. in social psychology from the University of Connecticut.

Dennis Fryback is professor emeritus in population health sciences and in industrial and systems engineering at the University of Wisconsin, Madison. He has specialized in methodological issues underpinning medical decision making, cost-effectiveness analysis of health care interventions, and health policy. He has headed projects on the evaluation of medical imaging technologies, computer simulation applied to understanding the natural history of breast cancer, application of Bayesian analysis to cost-effectiveness computations, and application of health-related quality of life measures to populations. He continues to conduct research using the public data set he helped to create, the U.S. National Health Measurement Study. He is a member of the Institute of Medicine. He has a Ph.D. in mathematical psychology from the University of Michigan.

David B. Grusky is professor of sociology at Stanford University, director of the Center for the Study of Poverty and Inequality, coeditor of *Pathways Magazine*, and coeditor of the Stanford University Press Social Inequality Series. His research addresses issues of inequality and takes on such questions as whether and why gender, racial, and class-based inequalities are growing stronger, why they differ in strength across countries, and how such changes and differences are best measured. He is a fellow of the American Association for the Advancement of Science, a recipient of the 2004 Max Weber Award, founder of the Cornell University Center for the Study of Inequality, and a former Presidential Young Investigator. He has M.S. and Ph.D. degrees in sociology from the University of Wisconsin, Madison.

Robert M. Hauser is executive director, Division of Behavioral and Social Sciences and Education at the National Research Council and Vilas Research Professor, Emeritus, at the University of Wisconsin, Madison. He has worked on the Wisconsin Longitudinal Study since 1969 and directed it since 1980. His current research interests include trends in educational progression and social mobility in the United States among racial and ethnic groups, the uses of educational assessment as a policy tool, the effects of families on social and economic inequality, and changes in socioeconomic standing, health, and well-being across the life course. He is a member of the National Academy of Sciences and has served on the National Research Council's Committee on National Statistics, Division of Behavioral and Social Sciences and Education, and Board on Testing and Assessment; he also has served on numerous research panels of the National Research Council and has chaired panel studies of high-stakes testing and standards for adult literacy. He has a B.A. in economics from the University of Chicago and M.A. and Ph.D. degrees in sociology from the University of Michigan.

Rick Hoyle is professor of psychology and neuroscience at Duke University, where he serves as associate director of the Center for Child and Family Policy and director of the Methodology and Statistics Core in the Transdisciplinary Prevention Research Center. The primary focus of his research is the study of basic cognitive, affective, and social processes involved in self-regulation. This research comprises two streams: one primarily involves controlled laboratory experiments focused on the social and psychological resources that enable successful self-regulation, and the other primarily involves correlational and field research focused on personality and social processes associated with failures of self-regulation as they manifest in problem behavior. He has a Ph.D. in psychology (social psychology program) from the University of North Carolina, Chapel Hill.

Sheila Jasanoff is Pforzheimer professor of science and technology studies at Harvard University's John F. Kennedy School of Government, where she directs the Program on Science, Technology, and Society. Her research focuses on the relationship of science and technology to law, politics, and policy in modern democratic societies, with particular emphasis on the role of science in cultures of public participation and public reasoning. She has written and lectured widely on environmental regulation, risk management, and the politics of the life sciences in the United States, Europe, and India. She has a Ph.D. in linguistics from Harvard University and a J.D. from Harvard Law School.

Rebecca A. Maynard is university trustee chair professor of education and social policy in the University of Pennsylvania's Graduate School of Education. Her work involves the design and conduct of rigorous randomized controlled trials in the areas of education and social policy, having overseen the design and implementation of dozens of experimental-design and multi-method evaluations of important programs and policies in both school and community settings. In recent years, she also has contributed to the development of practices for improving application of systematic review methods to education research, policy, and practice. She has a Ph.D. in economics from the University of Wisconsin, Madison.

Robert T. Michael is Eliakim Hastings Moore distinguished service professor emeritus in the Harris School of Public Policy Studies at the University of Chicago and project director of the National Longitudinal Studies Program of the National Opinion Research Center. His primary research interests are adult sexual behavior, investments in children, and the measurement of poverty. At the National Research Council, Michael chaired panels on pay equity research and on poverty and family assistance and served as a member of groups on children, youth, and families and the design of nonmarket accounts. He has a B.A. in economics and philosophy from Ohio Wesleyan University and a Ph.D. in economics from Columbia University.

Geoff Mulgan is director of the Young Foundation, a London-based center for social research, innovation, enterprise, and public policy with a 50-year history of pioneering sociological research and creating new organizations in the public, private, and nonprofit sectors. He is also a visiting professor at the London School of Economics and Political Science, University College London, and Melbourne University. Between 1997 and 2004 he had various roles in the U.K. government, including director of the government's Strategy Unit and head of policy in the prime minister's office. He also has been chief adviser to Member of Parliament Gordon Brown, a lecturer in telecommunications, an investment executive, and a reporter on BBC TV and radio. His most recent book is *The Art of Public Strategy*. He has a Ph.D. in telecommunications from the University of Westminster.

Robert A. Pollak is Hernreich distinguished professor of economics in the Faculty of Arts and Sciences and the Olin School of Business at Washington University in St. Louis. His research interests include the economics of the family, price and cost-of-living indexes, and environmental policy. At the National Research Council, he served on the Committee on National Statistics panel on cost-of-living indexes. From 1997 to 2007, Pollak cochaired the MacArthur Foundation Network on the Family and the Economy, an interdisciplinary group of economists, sociologists, and developmental psychologists studying the functioning of families. He has a Ph.D. in economics from the Massachusetts Institute of Technology.

Kenneth Prewitt is the Carnegie professor of public affairs and the vice-president for global centers at Columbia University. In addition to teaching for many years at the University of Chicago, he has served as the director of the U.S. Census Bureau, director of the National Opinion Research Center, president of the Social Science Research Council, and senior vice president of the Rockefeller Foundation. He is a lifetime National Associate of the National Research Council/National Academy of Sciences; a fellow of the American Academy of Arts and Sciences, the American Academy of Political and Social Science, the American Association for the Advancement of Science, the Center for the Advanced Study in the Behavioral Sciences, and the Russell-Sage Foundation; and member of other professional associations. He has an M.A. from Washington University, attended the Harvard Divinity School as a Danforth fellow, and has a Ph.D. in political science from Stanford University.

Barbara Schneider is the John A. Hannah distinguished professor in the College of Education and the Department of Sociology at Michigan State University. She worked for 18 years at the University of Chicago, holding positions as a professor in sociology and human development and as a senior researcher at the National Opinion Research Center. In her research, she uses a sociological lens to understand societal conditions and interpersonal interactions that create norms and values that enhance human and social capital. Her work focuses on how the social contexts of schools and families influence the academic and social well-being of adolescents as they move into adulthood. She has a Ph.D. from Northwestern University.

C. Matthew Snipp is the Burnet C. and Mildred Finley Wohlford professor in the Department of Sociology, director of the Center for the Comparative Study of Race and Ethnicity, and director of the Secure Data Center in the Institute for Research in the Social Sciences at Stanford University. His current research and writing deal with the methodology of racial measurement, changes in the social and economic well-being of American ethnic minorities, and American Indian education. He also has been involved with several advisory working groups evaluating the 2000 census and three National Research Council panels focused on the 2010 and 2020 censuses; has served as a member of the Board of Scientific Counselors of the Centers for Disease Control and Prevention and the National Center for Health Statistics; and served on the council of the Inter-University Consortium of Political and Social Research. He has a Ph.D. in sociology from the University of Wisconsin, Madison.

Miron L. Straf (*Study Director*) is deputy director of the Division of Behavioral and Social Sciences and Education at the National Research Council and study director of the division's project on the use of social science research as evidence in public policy. Previously he served as director of the division's Committee on National Statistics and at the National Science Foundation, where he worked on developing the research priority area for the social, behavioral, and economic sciences. He has also taught at the University of California, Berkeley, and the London School of Economics and Political Science. His major research interests are government statistics and the use of information for public policy decision making. He has a Ph.D. in statistics from the University of Chicago.

Jack E. Triplett has been with the Brookings Institution since 1997, currently as nonresident senior fellow. Previously, he has held the positions of chief economist at the U.S. Bureau of Economic Analysis, associate commissioner for research and evaluation at the Bureau of Labor Statistics, and assistant director for price monitoring at the U.S. Council on Wage and Price Stability. He has been particularly interested in methodological issues involved in estimating price, output, and productivity measures for high-tech products, including computers, and for other goods and services that exhibit rapid quality and technological improvements, including medical care. He has B.A, M.A., and Ph.D. degrees from the University of California, Berkeley.

John Robert Warren is professor of sociology at the University of Minnesota. In his ongoing research he is investigating methods for measuring high school completion rates, assessing the magnitude of panel conditioning biases in longitudinal surveys, modeling the impact of life-course trajectories of employment and family statuses on well-being in later adulthood, and studying the factors that lead voters to support school operating levies. He is coprincipal investigator on a project to harmonize, integrate, link, and disseminate all existing data from the Current Population Survey. He is also an investigator on the Wisconsin Longitudinal Study, which has followed members of the Wisconsin high school class of 1957 and their families over half a century. He has a Ph.D. from the University of Wisconsin, Madison.

Robert J. Willis is professor of economics and research professor in the Survey Research Center and the Population Studies Center of the Institute for Social Research. He is the past director of the Health and Retirement Study, a longitudinal survey of over 22,000 persons over age 50 in the United States, and currently directs a project on cognitive economics. His research involves the economics of the family, marriage, and fertility, labor economics, human capital, and population and economic development. He has a Ph.D. from the University of Washington.